TEESSIDE &
OLD CLEVELAND

THROUGH TIME

Robin Cook

AMBERLEY PUBLISHING

First published 2010

Amberley Publishing Plc
Cirencester Road, Chalford,
Stroud, Gloucestershire, GL6 8PE

www.amberley-books.com

Copyright © Robin Cook 2010

The right of Robin Cook to be identified as the Author
of this work has been asserted in accordance with the
Copyrights, Designs and Patents Act 1988.

ISBN 978 1 84868 392 1

British Library Cataloguing in Publication Data.
A catalogue record for this book is available from the
British Library.

Typeset in 10pt on 12pt Sabon.
Typesetting and Origination by FONTHILLDESIGN.
Printed in the UK.

Introduction

I make no apology for delivering a new volume of early photographs of the Teesside and Old Cleveland area. Much to the joy of the collectors, unusual and interesting postcards and early photographs of the district continue to turn up, although regrettably not as frequently or as cheaply as used to be the case. Whilst the public generally are not necessarily serious students of our local history in terms of scholarly studies and papers on the subject, they can always enjoy an attractive annotated picture book on the subject, providing it presents striking fresh images of our unknown past. The challenge is to find early views which have not been reproduced before and which lend themselves, as in this case, to being married up with a modern equivalent of the same subject. In some examples this is fairly simple. Taking a modern photograph from an identical camera position illustrates the buildings that have gone, or have since arrived, during the intervening years, which, as in the case of this selection, could be a period of more than a century. But in some cases it is not possible to take up the same camera position, due to buildings now standing where you want to position yourself in order to take the photograph — e.g. Whitby harbour side. And in some cases there has been such a change in the interim period that a compromise view has to be taken — e.g. The Black Bull Inn at Yarm.

The Teesside and Old Cleveland area represents a rewarding catchment because it includes such a wide range of subject material. The industrial heritage of Middlesbrough includes the Docks; the seaside resorts for holiday makers include Redcar, Saltburn, Staithes, and Whitby; the fishing industry includes Staithes and Whitby; the tourist attractions include pretty towns, villages and countryside, like Stokesley, Osmotherley and Bilsdale; and the local historians see interest in places like Stockton, Yarm, Middlesbrough, and Whitby. The challenge in providing information to accompany a selection of early pictures in a book like this one is to include enough information to make every page interesting, making sure that all the facts stated are accurate, and taking care that there is not too much text so that the reader becomes irritated by the format.

One of the learning experiences for me in putting together this book was getting used to operating for the first time a digital camera in order to take the modern photographs. This was in personal terms a new challenge, and had many problems. Quite apart from simply trying to take the best pictures from the right place, I learnt that modern traffic and car parking is no respecter of those seeking an interesting image in a place where there were no cars at all in the earlier postcard or photograph. Although being urged to get the best blue skies on all occasions, the weather had a happy knack of letting me down just at the key moment. And in some cases it made sense to try to capture a particular moment — e.g. the modern Yarm Fair in October compared with Yarm Fair long ago and the Saltburn cliff tram whilst it was still operating before its winter closure. I sadly failed, however, to get a Stokesley Fair picture on the right day in September. It's a case of spotting all these potential opportunities before the chance is gone for another year. A further learning experience in taking some of the street scenes was to discover how much more 'clutter' has been created by modern man in terms of bus shelters, lamp standards, traffic instructions, bollards and waste bins. Thoroughly depressing — I wonder if someone has the will to turn the clock back?

Three thank yous are highly appropriate for help provided in producing this book. To my collector friend John Armstrong who lent me a dozen of his best early postcards to fill out my own material. To Peter Dobing who understands the mysteries of linking digital cameras to computers considerably better than I do, and ensured thereby the high quality of the colour photographs. And to Joan Seymour whose professional skills on the computer keyboard transferred my accompanying text accurately into a form acceptable to the publisher!

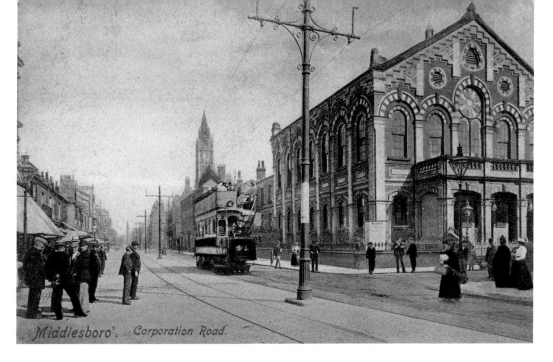

Middlesboro'. Corporation Road.

Corporation Road — Middlesbrough

The Wesleyan Chapel dominated Corporation Road from its opening in 1863. Known as 'Big Wesley', it seated a congregation of more than 800. Dating from about 1905, the early view also shows an open-topped tram with the town hall spire beyond it. The chapel was sold to British Home Stores in 1953, who built their present shop on the site. This whole area is now a pedestrian precinct.

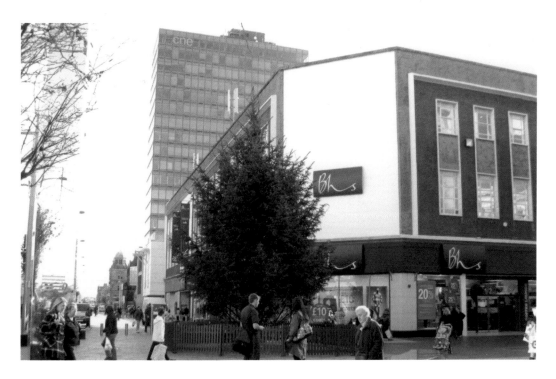

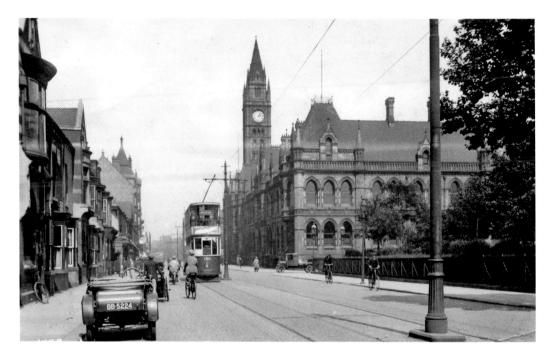

Albert Road

In the 1920s, the original town houses still survived on the left of the early view. This William Haig Parry postcard includes a period motor car and a tram on the Linthorpe to Transporter Bridge service, but the double-decker trams could not pass under the railway bridge at the station. The Cleveland Shopping Centre replaced the houses on the left, and the Corporation Hotel beyond them, in the 1970s.

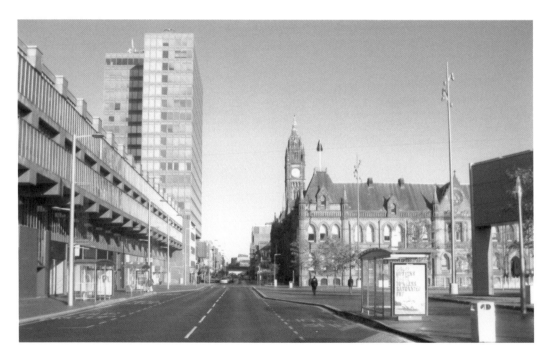

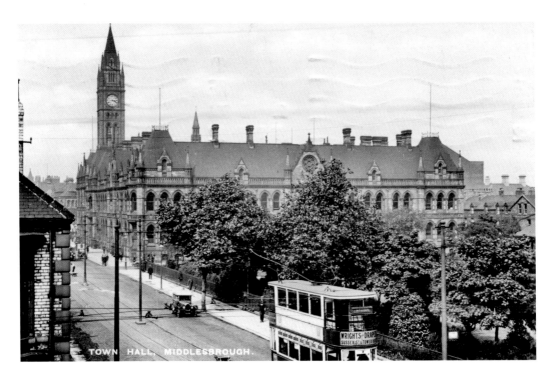

Town Hall

The town hall was opened by the Prince and Princess of Wales in January 1889, amidst spectacular ceremony. The adjacent Victoria Square — tree lined in its earlier years — was completed in 1901. The last tram on this route was in 1934, which signalled the end of tramways on Teesside. The town hall still stands proud today, but its surroundings have changed dramatically.

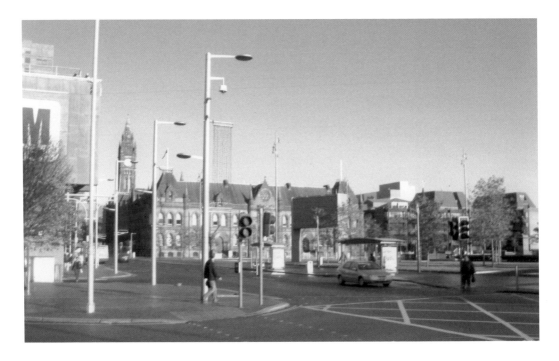

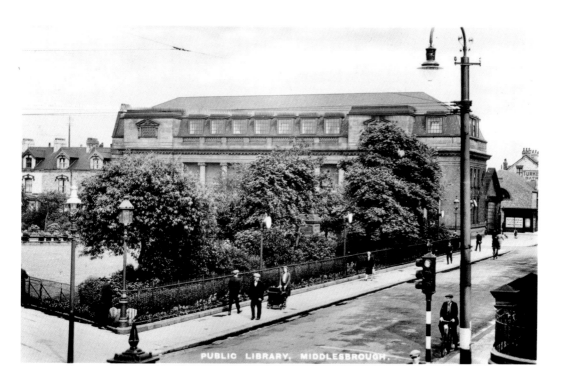

Public Library

This beautiful building — opened in 1912 — was the result of a generous grant from the Andrew Carnegie Foundation in the USA, which paid for the provision of a number of libraries in some of the urban communities in the United Kingdom. Standing in Dunning Road, it adjoined a row of terrace houses. The early view is from the 1930s, but modern thinking has opened out this area and pedestrianised Grange Road.

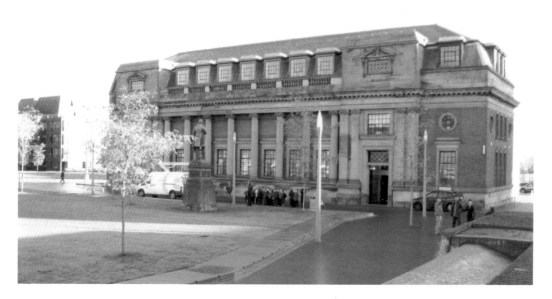

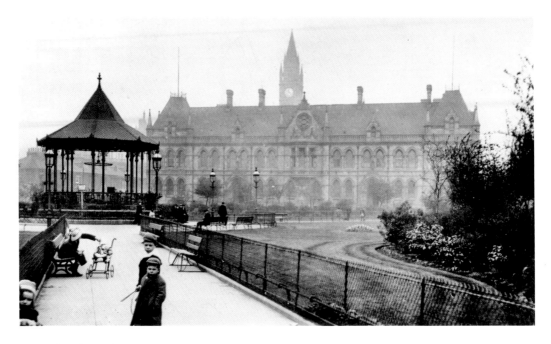

Victoria Park

The Band of the Coldstream Guards played in the new bandstand when Victoria Square was opened on 12 July 1901, with 1,500 guests taking tea with local Member of Parliament Colonel Sadler (later to be mayor) and his wife. Seats for the elderly were installed in 1906. Over the years, this area has changed its name and layout many times. Currently known as Central Square, it is an important open space for the town.

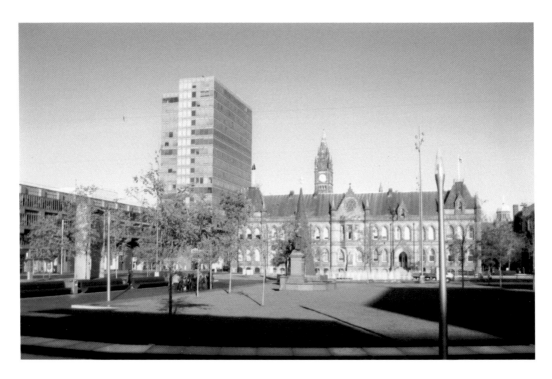

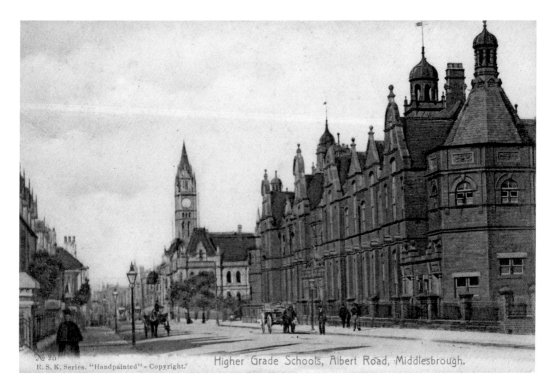

Higher Grade Schools, Albert Road, Middlesbrough.

Nº 25
R. S. K. Series. "Handpainted" - Copyright.

Hugh Bell Schools

Known at its opening in 1892 as Grange Road Schools, this early building became the Hugh Bell Schools in 1898 and then in 1907 was denoted as a Higher Grade School, at that time the only fee-paying school under the local Board of Education. An attractive building, it finally closed its doors in 1969 and was replaced by the much plainer Teesside Law Courts building.

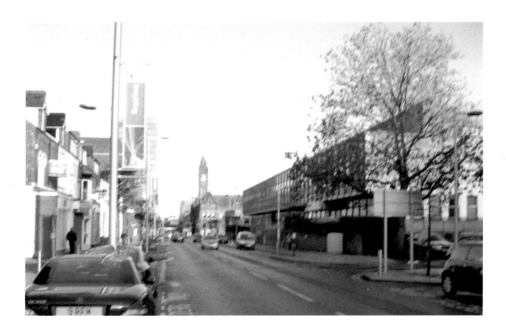

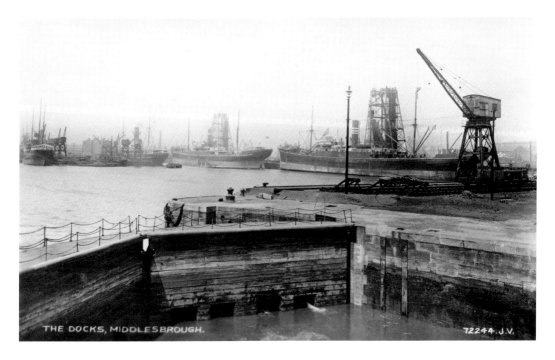

THE DOCKS, MIDDLESBROUGH.   72244.J.V.

Middlesbrough Docks

The original docks were constructed and first operated in the 1840s, and were progressively extended over the years as the local economy rose sharply, with much larger facilities for the later major industries being developed down river. This is a peaceful area now, with the new Middlesbrough College and the Riverside Football Stadium dominating the scene, but with the open water still thankfully preserved.

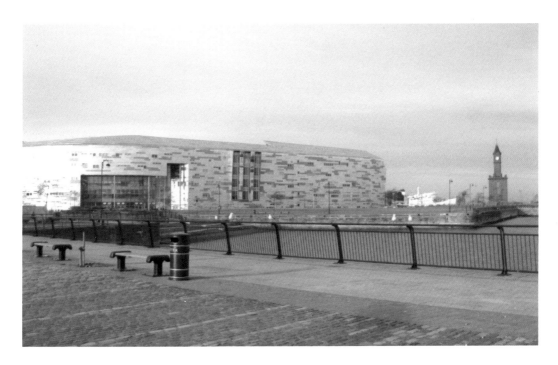

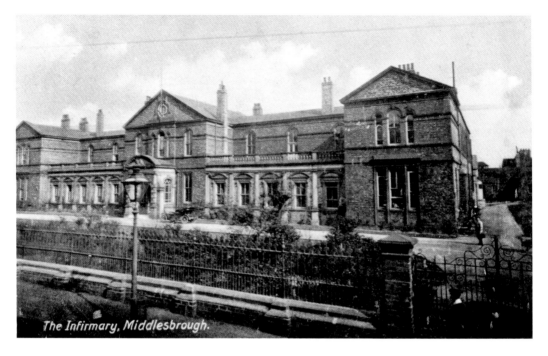

The Infirmary, Middlesbrough.

North Riding Infirmary

The infirmary was held in great affection by the local population. It opened in 1864 and was located on Newport Road, near to the Ironmasters District, to respond in part to industrial accidents. Mr H. W. F. Bolckow donated £5,000 of its total cost of £7,865. It later became a specialist ear, eye, nose and throat hospital but closed due to re-organisation within the last decade. Amid much controversy, it was demolished and a supermarket and hotel built. The original portico was preserved on site.

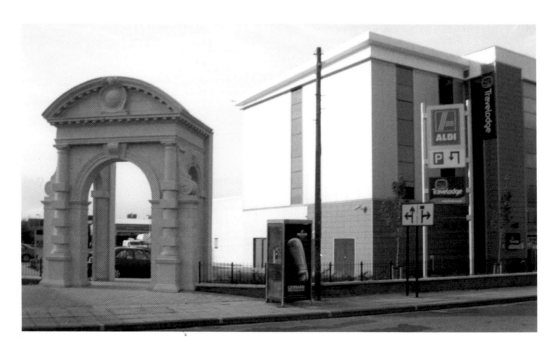

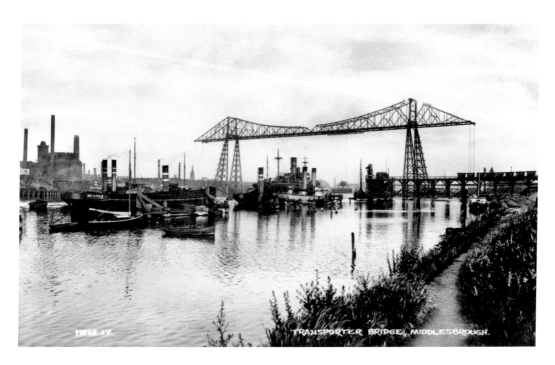

Transporter Bridge

The Transporter Bridge, which opened in 1911, allowed big vessels to be built higher upriver and cargo ships to pass through to Stockton. Its hanging carriage design was popular world wide from about 1890-1920. The early view is from the 1920s. This part of the river is now less busy — the commerce is further down river — but the bridge remains the symbol of the town of Middlesbrough, and it still provides a crossing point for vehicles and pedestrians.

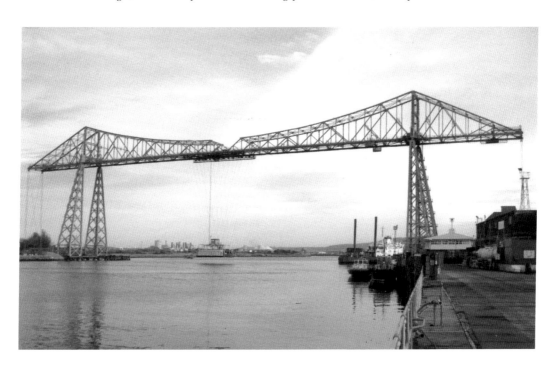

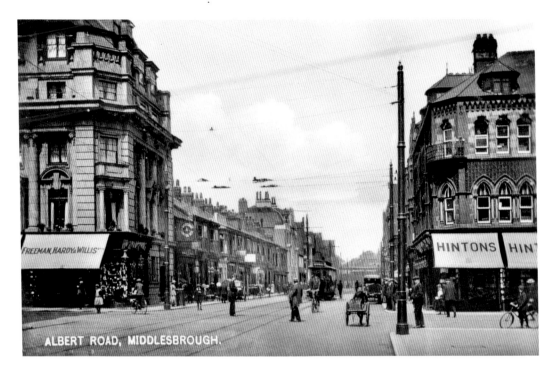

Albert Road

In the 1920s, a mixture of terrace houses and business properties shared the length of Albert Road. On the first floor of Hinton's grocery store there was a fashionable café. The railway station bridge can just be seen in the distance. This area is now entirely consisting of banks, restaurants and pubs and other commercial enterprises, and has been much re-developed.

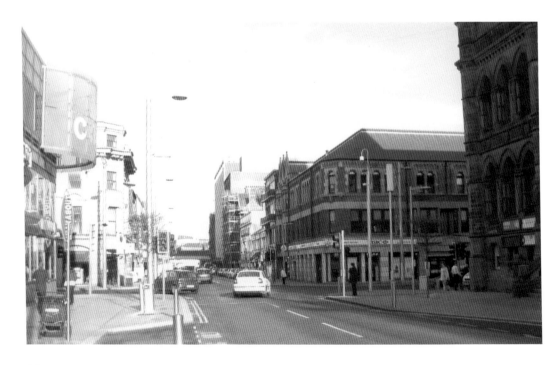

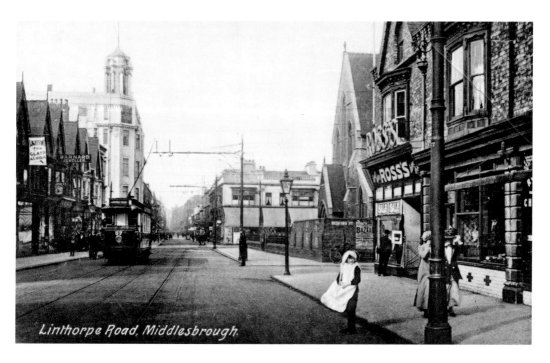

Linthorpe Road, Middlesbrough.

Linthorpe Road

The early postcard view is from about 1910, with the attractive Wright's Tower House in white stone on the left — now replaced by a modern branch of McDonalds. All Saints' church on the right was consecrated in 1878, and its most famous priest, Revd J. S. L. Burn, was there from 1884-1925. He remained a controversial figure within the Anglican Church throughout, though doing many good works amongst the poor.

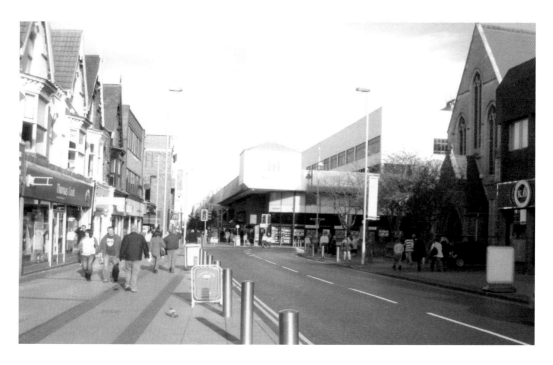

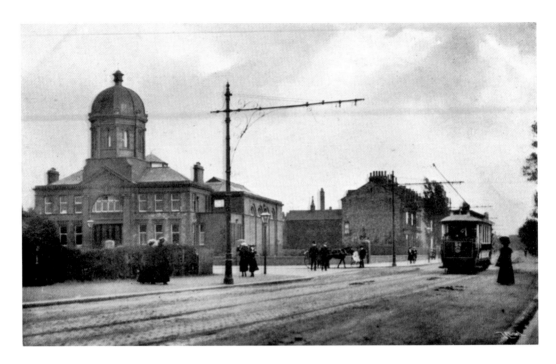

Dorman Museum

Opened in 1904 by his father Sir Arthur Dorman in memory of Lieutenant G. L. Dorman and his men of the Green Howards Regiment who were killed in the South African Boer Wars, the Dorman Museum stands near to the entrance to Albert Park, off Linthorpe Road. A new traffic-free precinct has recently been created in the area, which also contains the principal war memorials of Middlesbrough.

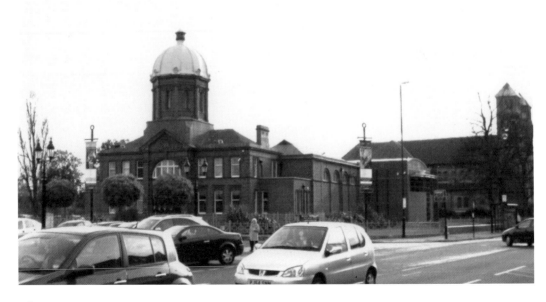

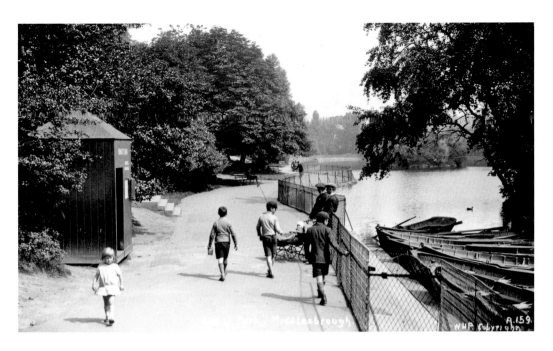

Albert Park — The Lake

The early postcard dates from the 1920s and was taken by William Haig Parry. The presence of the young children and the rowing boats add interest, as does the office on the left of the boat hirer. Given to the town by H. F. W. Bolckow, Albert Park was formally opened in 1868 by Prince Arthur, son of Queen Victoria, and named after his father. Recently refurbished, the park remains an important open space for Middlesbrough's residents and visitors.

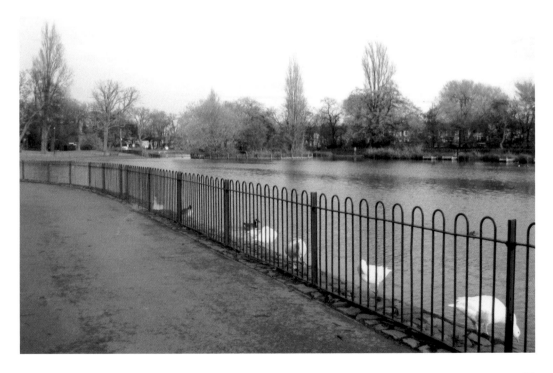

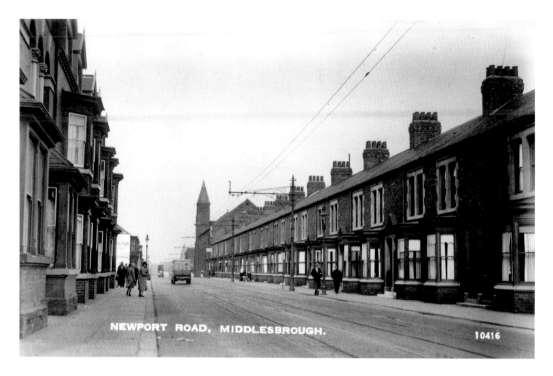

NEWPORT ROAD, MIDDLESBROUGH.   10416

Newport Road

This was a superior residential area when the early view was taken in the 1920s, notwithstanding the tramlines linking Middlesbrough and Stockton. The tower of St Cuthbert's church can be seen in the Middlesbrough direction. Later, light industrial developments replaced all the houses seen on the left-hand side of the earlier scene.

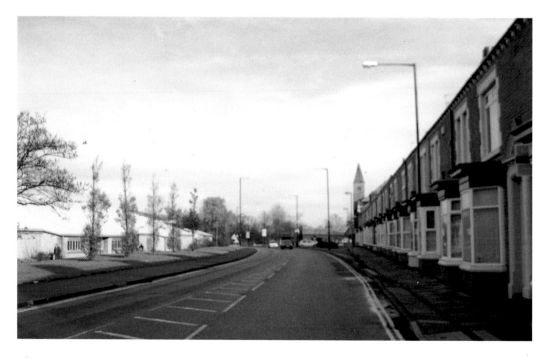

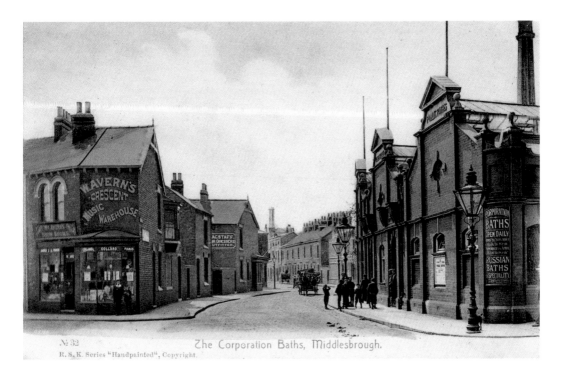

No 32

The Corporation Baths, Middlesbrough.

R. S. K. Series "Handpainted", Copyright.

Gilkes Street Swimming Baths

The Corporation Baths, which opened in 1884, in Gilkes Street, off Linthorpe Road, were famous for their links with the Hatfield family. Father was the baths' superintendent, and son Jack swam in the 1912 Olympic Games and won two silver medals. In recent years, the whole area has been re-developed and is now covered by the Captain Cook Square shopping centre.

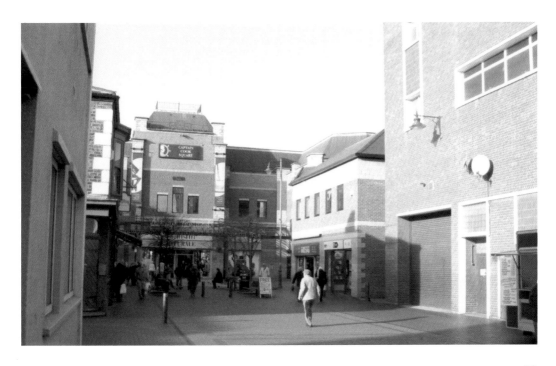

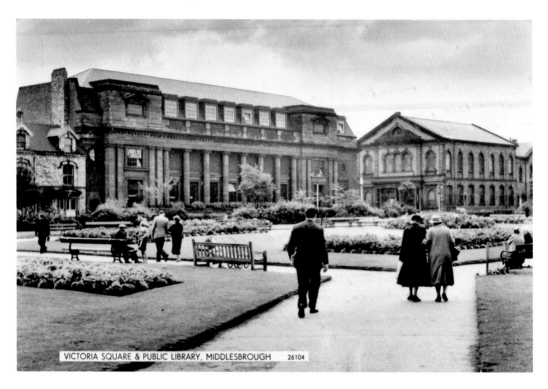

VICTORIA SQUARE & PUBLIC LIBRARY, MIDDLESBROUGH 26104

Library and Methodist Church

Until 1960, the Grange Road Methodist Church stood at the corner of Victoria Square, across the road from the Carnegie Library. The church had been purchased by the Corporation in 1935 but was demolished in 1960, and in 1962 a new police headquarters was opened on the site, built in the 'modern' style. That new building has now been empty for more than a year and has just been demolished.

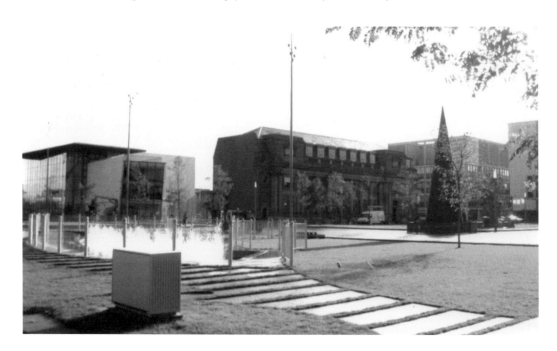

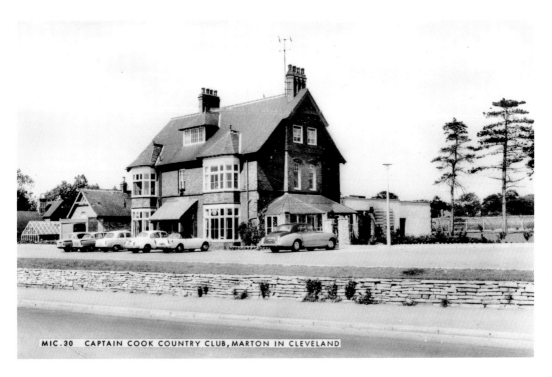

MIC.30 CAPTAIN COOK COUNTRY CLUB, MARTON IN CLEVELAND

Marton Country Club

The original substantial house, which had been converted into the Captain Cook Country Club, was later replaced by a large but characterless building more suited to be a large entertainment venue — the Marton Country Club. The earlier postcard probably dates from the 1960s and shows various outbuildings and even a greenhouse!

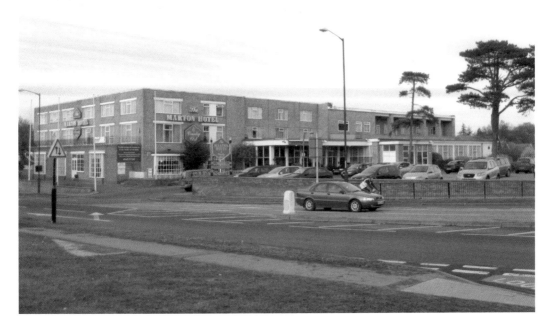

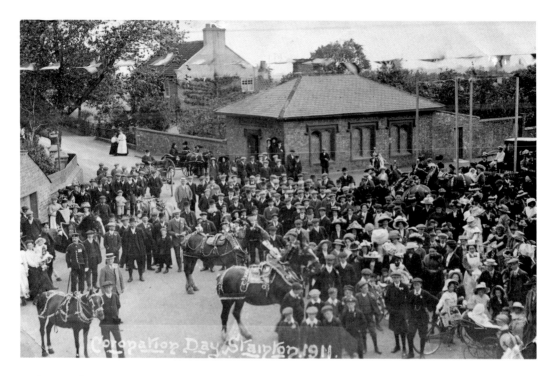

Stainton Village

Stainton lies just to the south of Middlesbrough, close to the Parkway arterial road. Most of the village must have turned out on the occasion of the 1911 coronation of George V, and an old farmhouse can be seen behind the mullioned window village hall, built originally as the National School in 1844 but enlarged and converted in 1922 to a memorial hall.

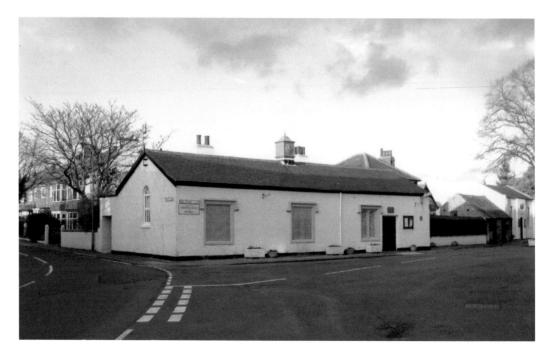

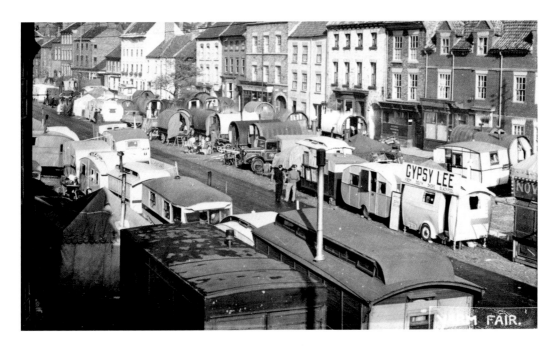

Yarm Fair

The October fair at Yarm began as a horse dealing occasion centuries ago. It also became an important cheese-trading event in the nineteenth century and later. The earlier High Street view is from the 1940s with traditional Romany vardoes in the background. A few of these still appear today, but the other caravans have become much more stylish, as have the roundabouts and massive thrill machines.

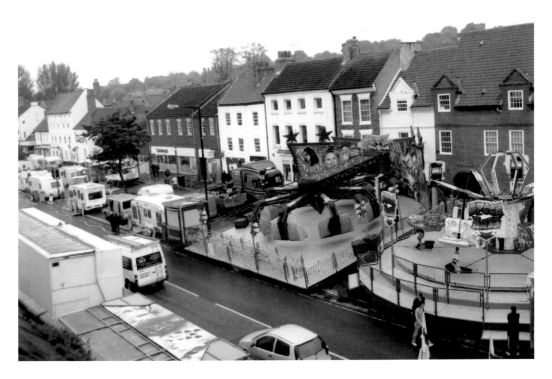

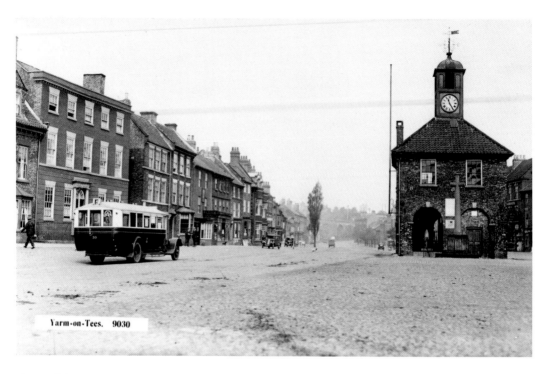

Yarm-on-Tees. 9030

Yarm High Street

An early Stockton Corporation bus stands in front of Eastry House, a splendid period residence in Yarm High Street, where many three-storey eighteenth-century town houses can still be seen. With difficulty, five other vehicles can just be made out in the 1920's view. The traffic scene is sadly very different today, when the motor car has become the bane of this attractive award-winning town. Extensive cobblestones are a feature of the wide street.

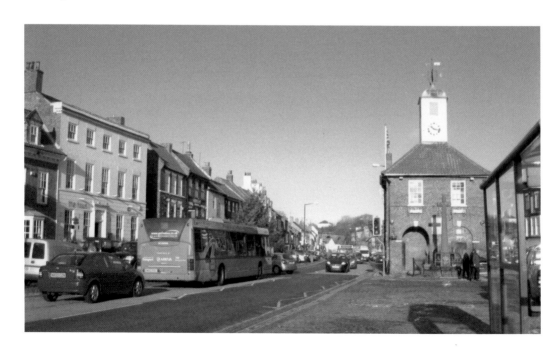

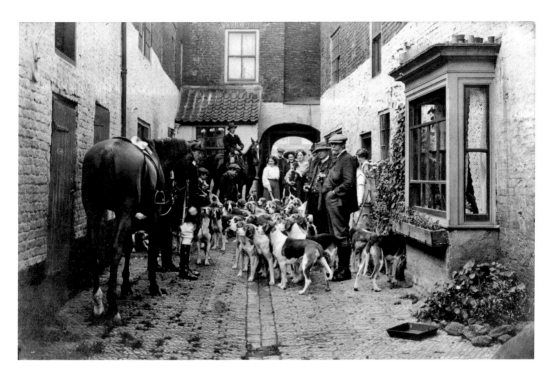

Black Bull Inn Yard

Many of the poorer Yarm residents lived up the yards off the High Street in earlier days. The great majority of the yards have now gone, including the one illustrated, which was incorporated within the lounge bar of the Black Bull Inn. The Hurworth Hunt is seen assembling for the preliminary stirrup cup in 1910. Some of the houses in the few remaining yards are now very fashionable places to live. Foxes may still roam the town!

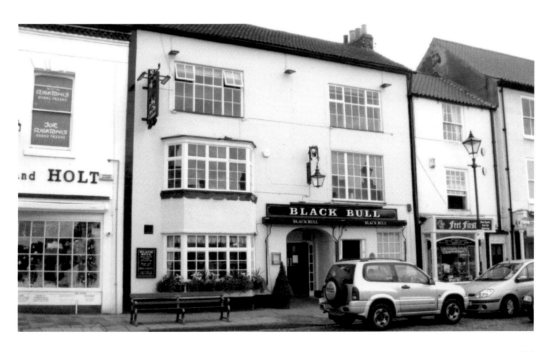

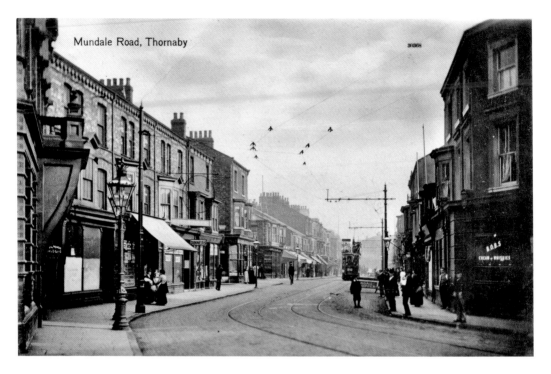

Mundale Road, Thornaby

Mandale Road, Thornaby on Tees
A postcard view of Mandale Road, Thornaby on Tees, with a small section of the attractive town hall on the extreme left. This was a busy shopping area in an industrial district of shipbuilding, blast furnaces and engineering works. Known earlier as South Stockton, Thornaby lay across the River Tees in the North Riding of Yorkshire and gained its Borough Charter in 1892.

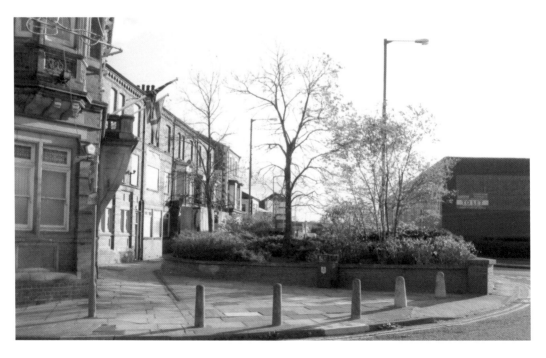

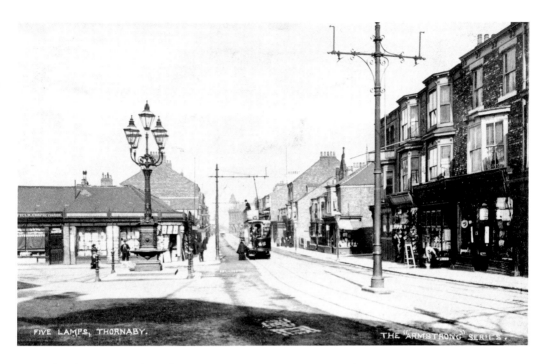

The Five Lamps, Thornaby on Tees

One of the many different postcard views of the Five Lamps road junction in Thornaby, which dates from about 1905. Famous for its range of small and interesting shops, this public square was the centre of much social activity. Thornaby Town Hall can just be seen in the distance, beyond the tram. This area — part of Stockton Council since 1974 — is now very run down, comprising mainly derelict car showrooms and empty properties. Note the modern five lamps in the foreground.

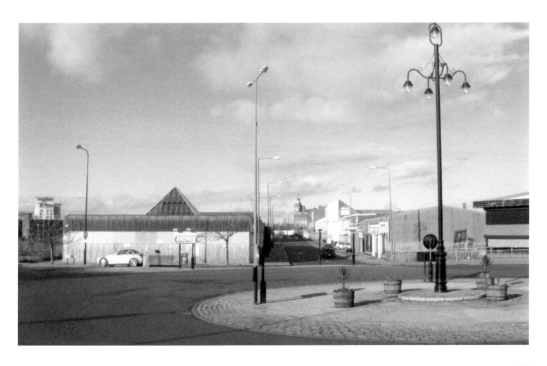

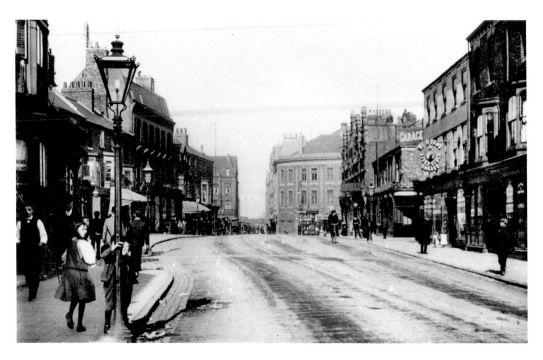

Yarm Lane, Stockton on Tees

An attractive early view — about 1910 — of Yarm Lane in Stockton, with the High Street crossing the picture at the far end. The new Castle Theatre faces us in the centre, now the site of the abandoned Swallow Hotel. The old street gas lamps had so much more character than their modern equivalents, and this area was much more thriving and tidy than it appears today.

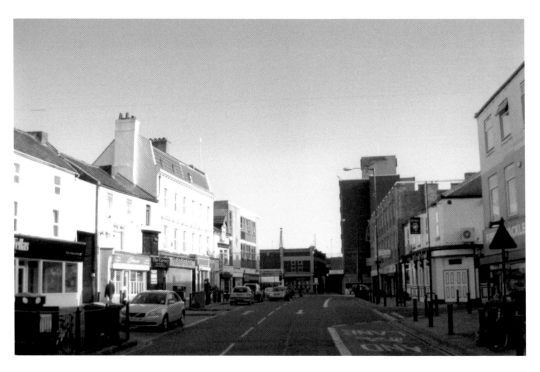

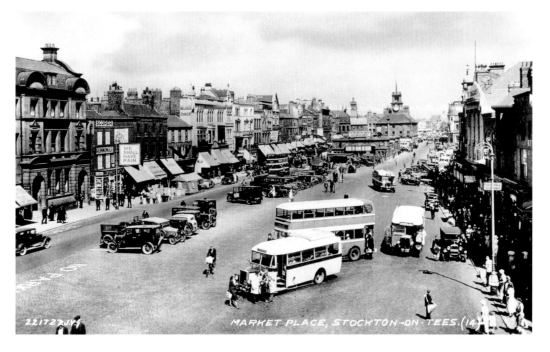

High Street, Stockton on Tees

Looking northwards up Stockton High Street towards the town hall, the cars and buses on the earlier view recall the 1930s when life was lived at a different pace. Note all the sun blinds on the east facing shops. In keeping with modern planning policies, this very wide High Street now has traffic restrictions placed upon it for pedestrian safety reasons. Barclays Bank is the imposing period building on the left edge of the scene.

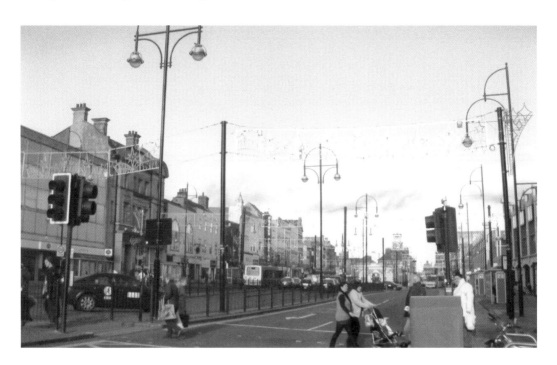

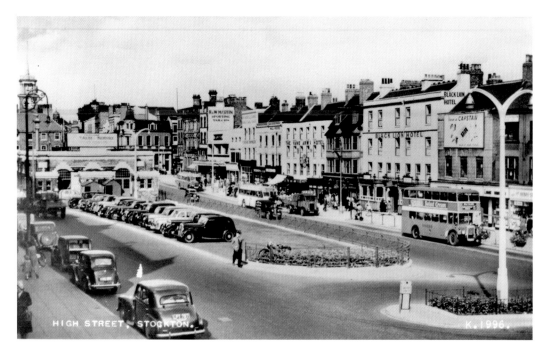

High Street, Stockton on Tees
Showing the splendid building façades on the East Side of Stockton High Street, with the historic Black Lion and Vane Arms Coaching Inns evident in the 1950s. The low Shambles Meat Market building can be seen on the left behind the row of parked cars, with the town hall just visible at the extreme left. The Council flattened these East Side buildings in the early 1970s in an act of legalised vandalism.

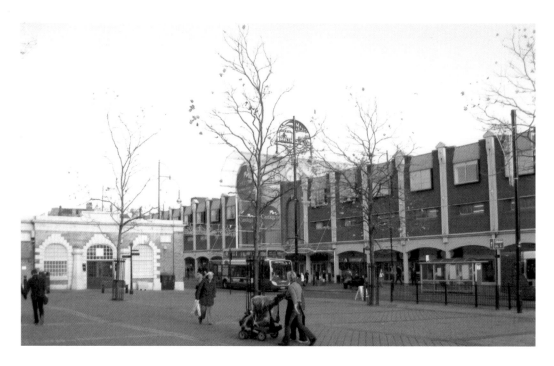

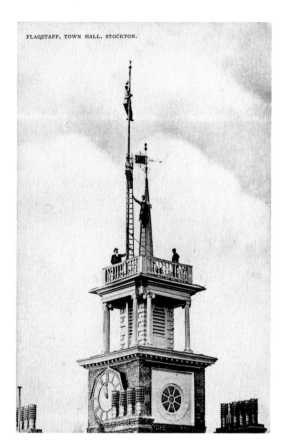

FLAGSTAFF, TOWN HALL, STOCKTON.

Stockton on Tees — the Town Hall

An unusual view of the tower of Stockton Town Hall, on a postcard dated 1905, with a group of five men using a ladder presumably to attach an appropriate flag to the very tall flagstaff. It looks quite precarious! The town hall was built in 1735 and dominates the High Street by its size and position.

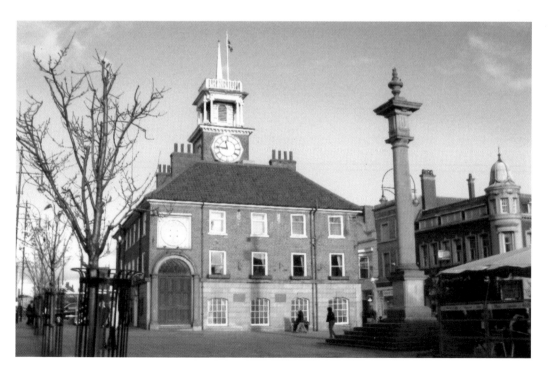

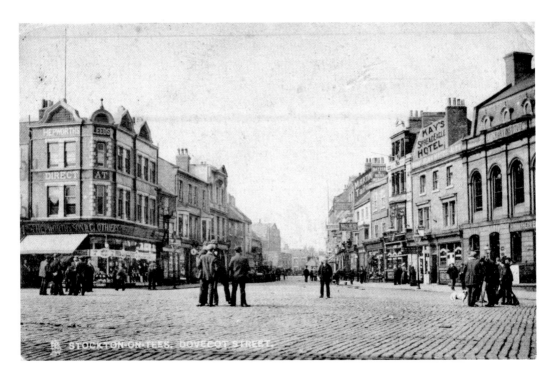

Dovecot Street, Stockton on Tees

Showing the entrance to Dovecot Street from the High Street, with the view from 1907 including the Literary Institute building on the extreme right and the Hepworths of Leeds clothing shop on the left, the latter building still there today. The High Street cobblestones can clearly be seen. The Alma Hotel and Kay's Spread Eagle Hotel lie just beyond the Literary Institute. There are fewer pubs today, but more clubs and bars, unheard of a hundred years ago.

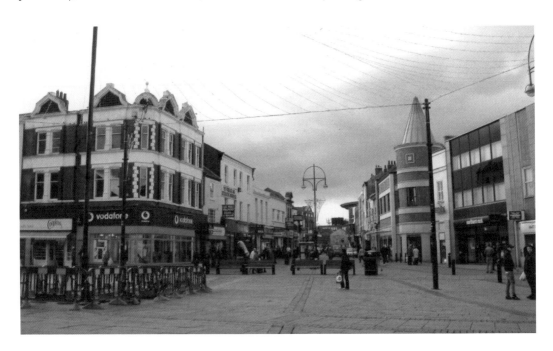

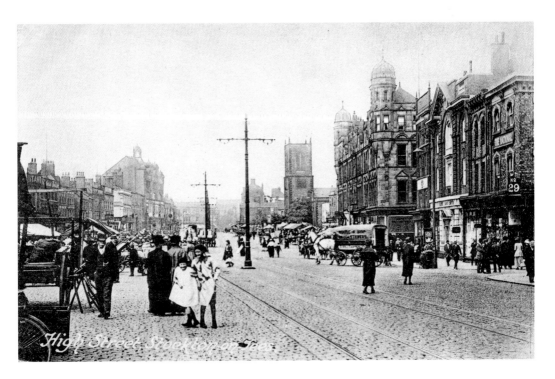

High Street — North End — Stockton on Tees

The early view dates from about 1905, showing a busy High Street with market stalls along the left side. The tallest building on the right with two towers — the Victoria Buildings — was demolished about 1964 and replaced by a very ordinary office block with ground floor shops. The centre building on the right — looking like a cinema front — was Lloyds Bank and still survives. The horse-drawn delivery cart belonged to the High Street store of Hill Carters — 'Drapers and Art Furnishers'.

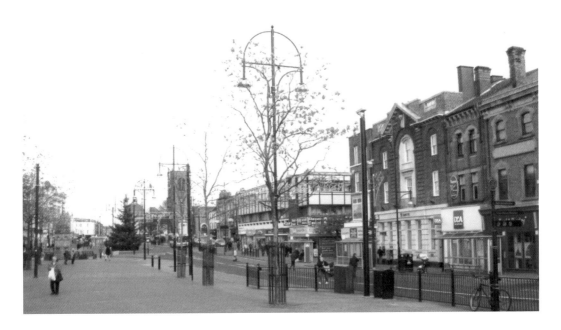

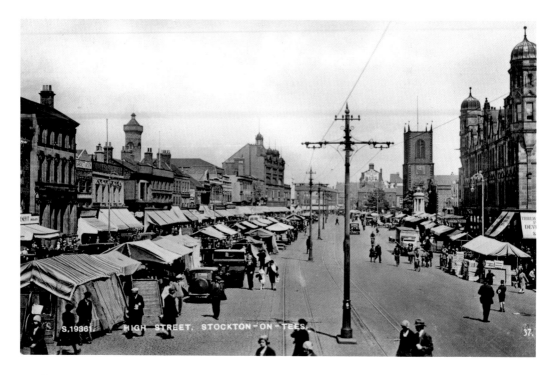

Stockton on Tees — the Market

A view from 1938 of the famous historic Stockton Market, with the Victoria Buildings on the right and the parish church beyond. The market has always been a feature of the High Street, although in modern times it has faced serious competition from cheap shops and may also have been affected by various re-designs of the High Street layout arising from pedestrian measures. The tall building centre left was Robinson's Coliseum department store — now Debenhams.

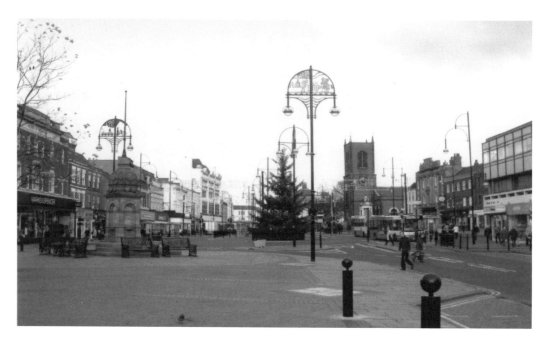

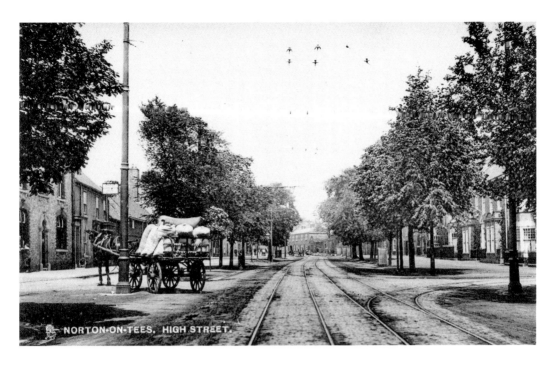

Norton on Tees — High Street

A tree-lined Norton High Street with the tram lines much in evidence. This route led from Norton Green through Stockton to North Ormesby, Middlesbrough. The lines lead off to the right into the local tram depot. The horse-drawn cart carries some substantial sacks. The High Street still maintains its historic atmosphere and charm today.

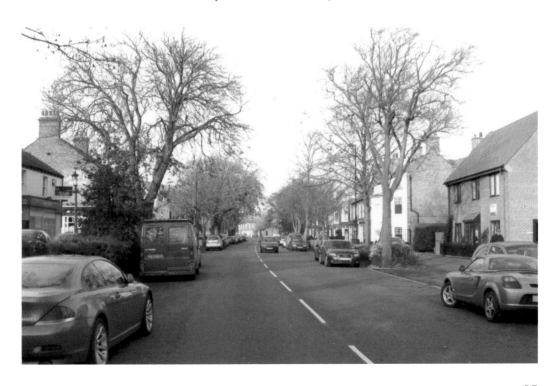

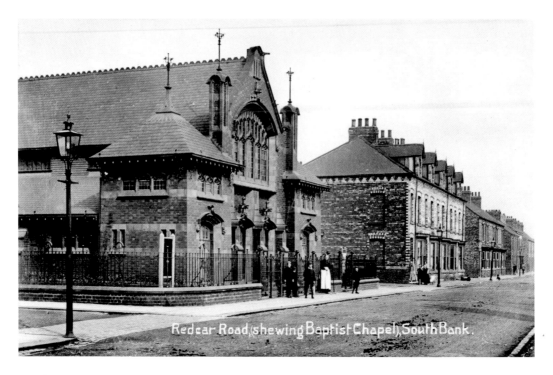

Redcar Road (shewing Baptist Chapel), South Bank.

South Bank — Baptist Chapel

The imposing Baptist Chapel in Redcar Road, South Bank, in 1912, with good quality terrace homes beyond. This attractive building opened in 1906 and is evidence of the wide range of places of worship provided for a believing community at that time. Sadly, few of the important buildings remain now in South Bank, and much of the housing has also gone, but the chapel building is still standing.

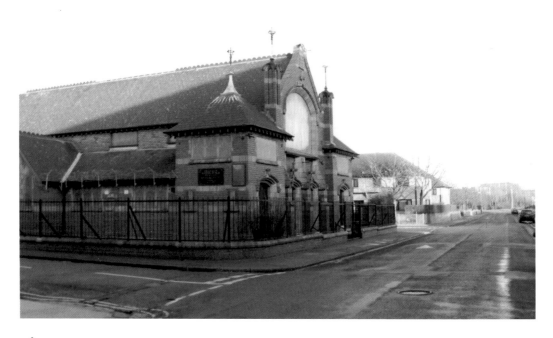

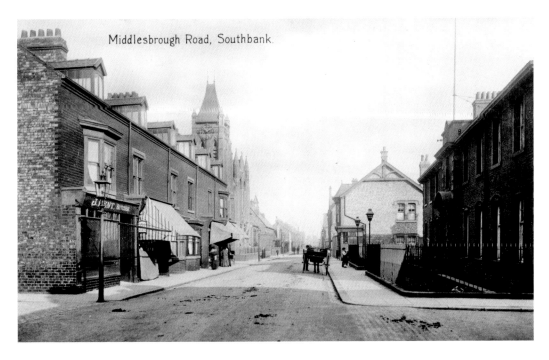

Middlesbrough Road, Southbank.

South Bank — Middlesbrough Road

The early postcard shows the famous St Peter's Roman Catholic church on the left centre, built in 1905, and the local police station in the right foreground. There was a strong immigrant Catholic community in the neighbourhood, with the men working in the local iron industry. The future of areas like South Bank remains a problem for the town planners, with many of the people and the buildings already no longer there.

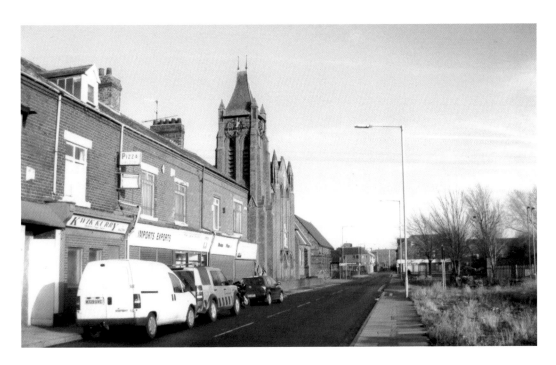

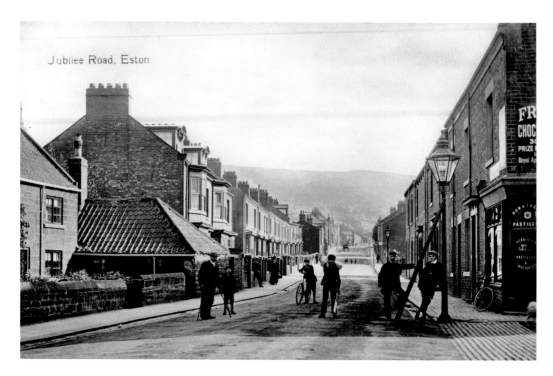

Jubilee Road, Eston

A ladder indicates possible repairs to an elegant gas lamp at the bottom of Jubilee Road in Eston. The ironstone bearing hills can be seen in the distance, and the shop on the right corner advertises Rowntree's Pastilles and Fry's chocolate. This early postcard is from about 1910.

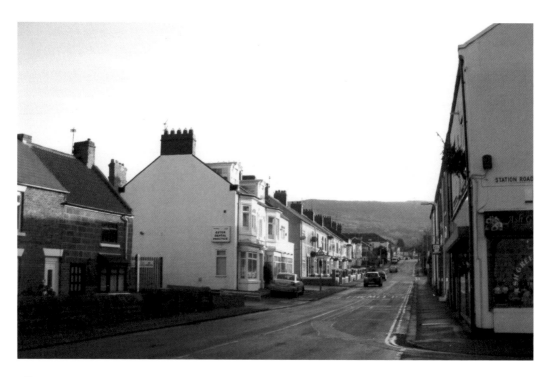

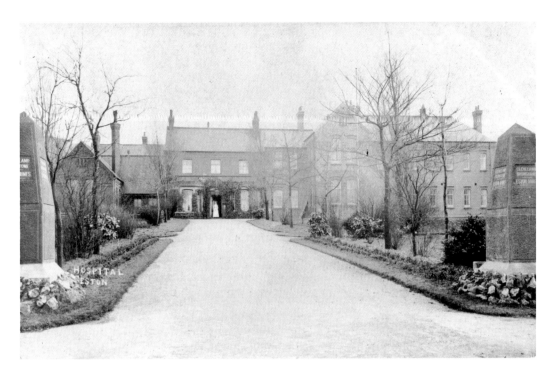

Miners' Hospital, Eston High Street

The Ironstone Miners' Hospital was built by Bolckow and Vaughan in 1884, originally for iron industry casualties but later for the whole community. It was eventually demolished in 1981 as the older small hospitals on Teesside began to be closed. The two symbolic solid ironstone gate pillars in the foreground were preserved and re-erected on the site in 2004.

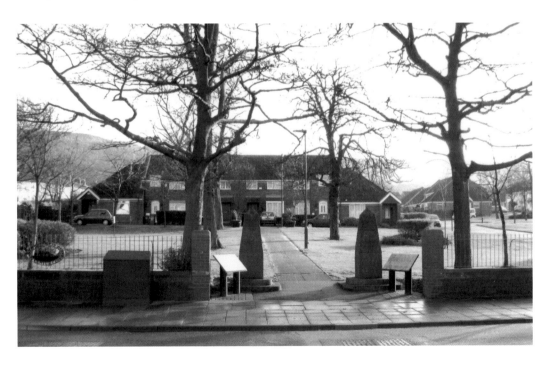

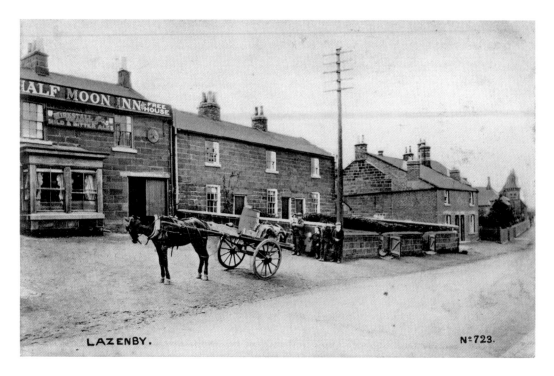

The Half Moon Inn, Lazenby

A peaceful scene outside the Half Moon Inn at Lazenby, beyond Eston. Some children watch a small delivery cart outside the pub whilst the horse stands patiently for its owner to return — possibly having a quick pint? A sign on the pub wall declares 'Kirkstall Company's Celebrated Mild and Bitter Ales', presumably brewed in Leeds for this free house.

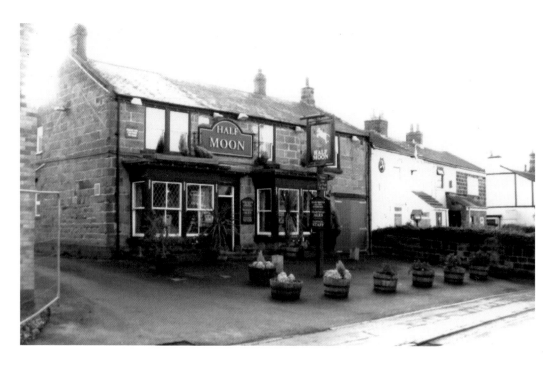

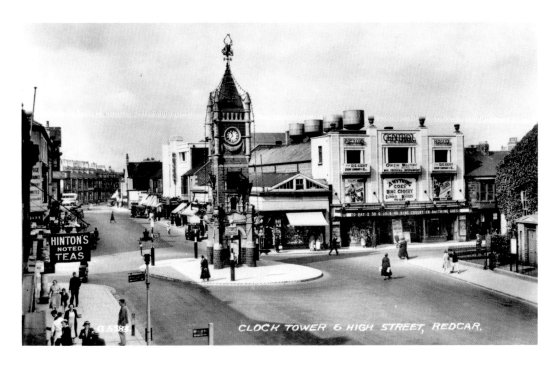

Redcar — the Clock Tower

A postcard view of the familiar Clock Tower in the centre of Redcar that was completed in 1912 in memory of King Edward VII. To the right is the old Central Picture House showing *Anything Goes* with Bing Crosby and Ida Lupino, probably in the mid-1940s. The cinema was destroyed by fire in the late 1940s. The white Regent Dance Hall can be seen in the distance to the left of the Clock Tower but is no longer there.

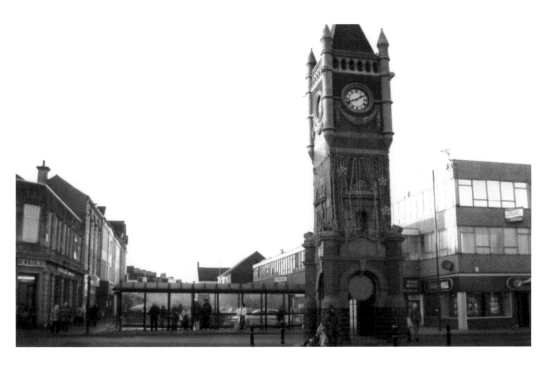

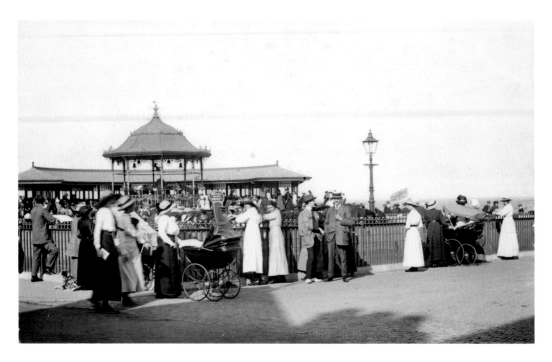

Redcar — the Bandstand

The Bandstand on the sea front was built in 1905. There is a band playing in this Edwardian view, the ladies look elegant in their long white summer dresses, and this enclosure was favoured by the children's nannies with their prams. Beyond the nearer pram can be seen a Nestlé's chocolate dispensing machine. What a contrast with the present scene!

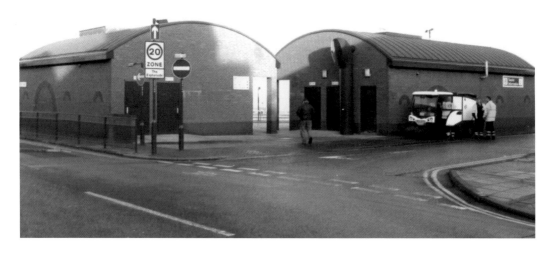

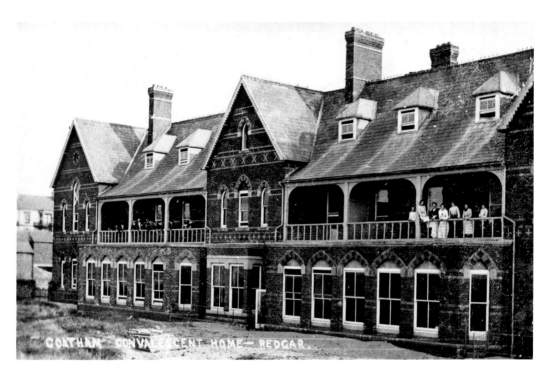

Redcar — the Coatham Convalescent Home

The substantial Coatham Convalescent Home is well illustrated here, with some of the staff and patients standing on the balconies at both ends. Opened in 1861, it was eventually demolished in 1957. Coal miners from County Durham were amongst its main clients. The much less attractive Redcar Bowl building was later erected on the same site.

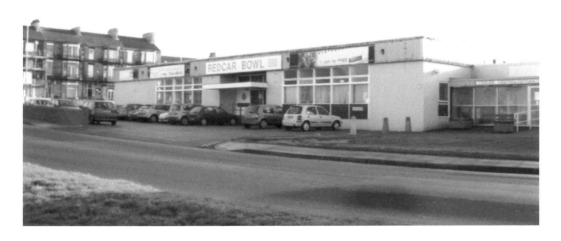

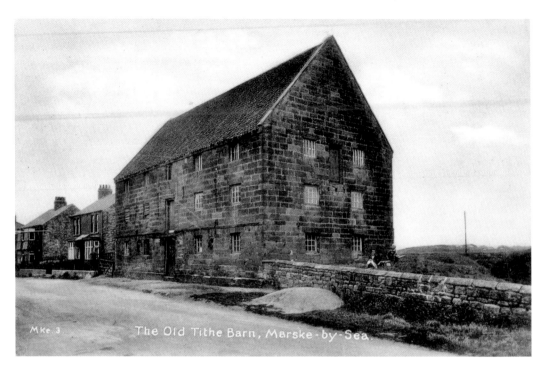

Marske-by-the-Sea — the Old Tithe Barn

A dominating relic of early Marske — the old 'Tithe Barn'. Little seems to be recorded of its origins or early ownership, but it was probably built in the eighteenth century as an exporting granary for the local Dundas Estate. Some time after this early postcard view was taken in the 1930s, the building was significantly modified and the roof lowered.

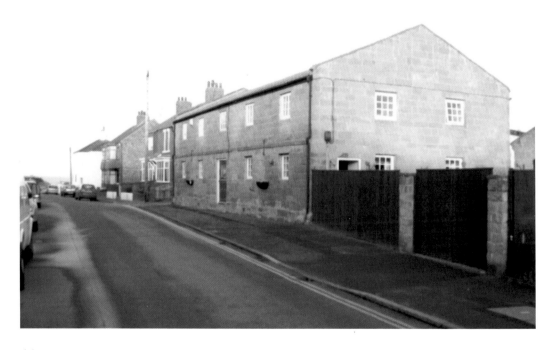

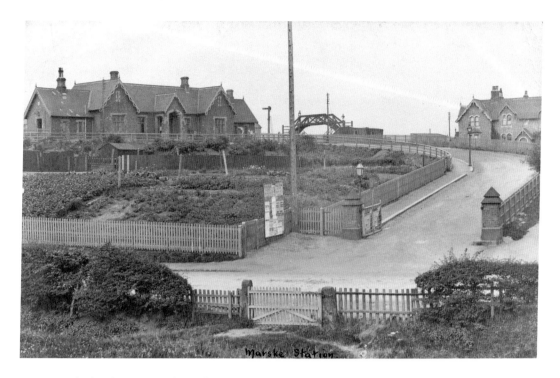

Marske Station.

Marske-by-the-Sea — The Railway Station

Posted in 1903, this view shows the approach road to the railway station at Marske, a much more developed travel facility at that time. The railway came to Marske in 1861, and the Station Master's house, seen on the right, also dates from that time. Many people depended on the early railways — there were few buses or family cars — but some of our surviving local railway stations do now seem neglected.

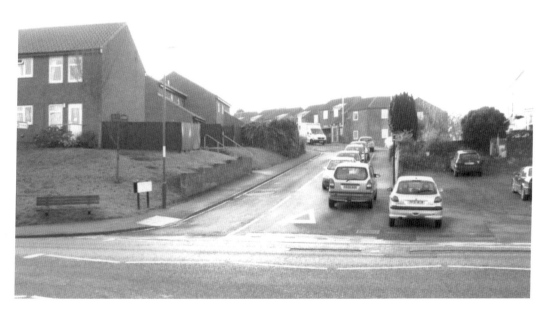

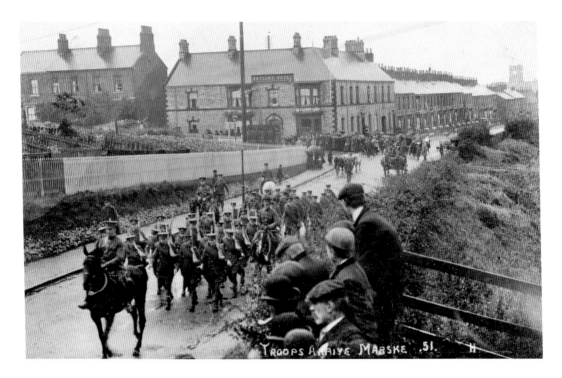

Marske-by-the-Sea — Military Exercises
Marske Railway Station lies off to the left, and the soldiers have just arrived by train for military exercises in the area in the years before the Great War. The Zetland Hotel dominates the rear centre, and the parish church tower can just be seen in the distance on the right. A small crowd by the hotel watch whilst sheltering under their umbrellas.

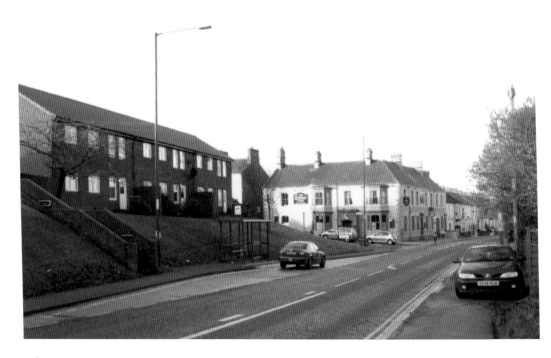

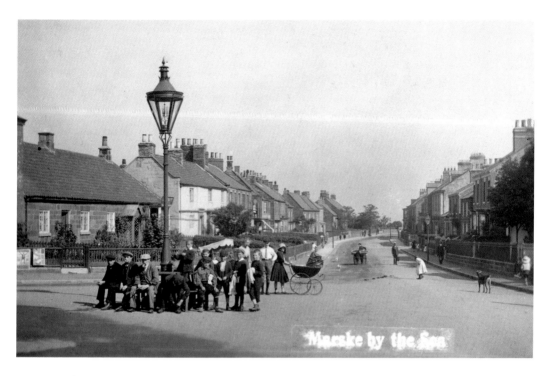

Marske-by-the-Sea — The High Street

Evidently it was safe to sit in the middle of the main road junction in about 1910! Looking seawards down the High Street, a group of local citizens watch the photographer as he composes his latest postcard. The passing traffic now causes much greater anxiety for the pedestrians, who are glad of the crossing points.

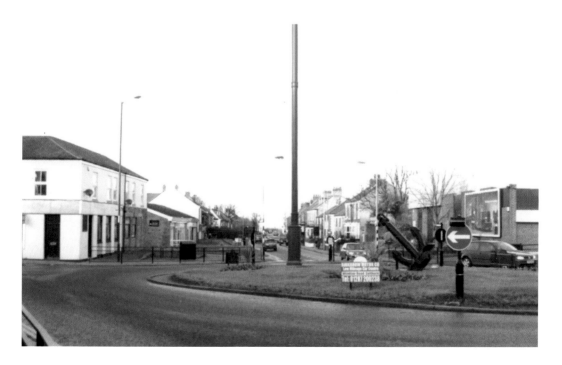

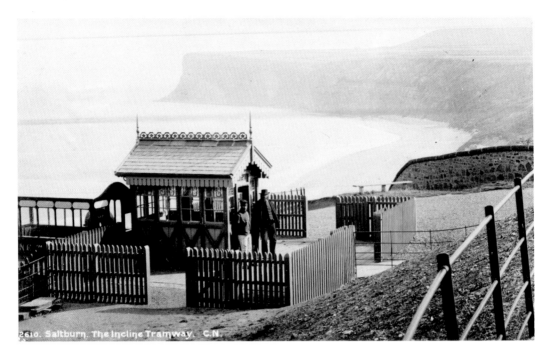

Saltburn — The Cliff Tram

A fine view at the top station of Saltburn's famous cliff tramway, opened in 1884 to replace a 'vertical hoist' down to the pier and beach, and still operating today. The motive power required arises from the pumping of water ballast into tanks on the two balanced carriages. One of the carriages can be seen on the left of the early picture, dating from 1905. More than 100,000 passengers now use the tram each season. The familiar outline of Huntcliff can be seen in the background.

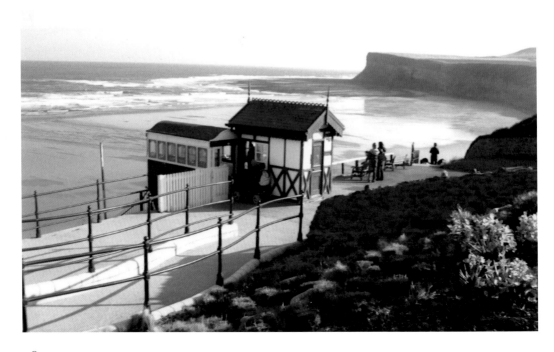

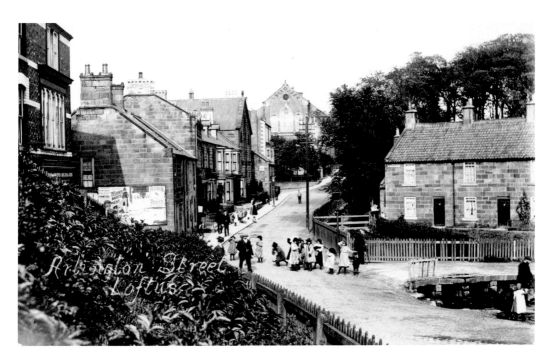

Loftus — Arlington Street

One of the largest communities in the East Cleveland towns and villages, Loftus has known varying fortunes as industries have come and gone — alum, ironstone, chemicals and potash, for example. It has an ancient history, but the closure of the local ironstone mine in 1958 was a particular body blow. Children playing in the street create a pleasant impression of life a century ago. Arlington Street is part of the High Street, heading out towards Staithes.

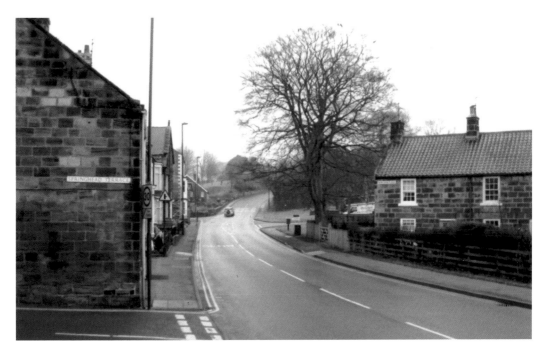

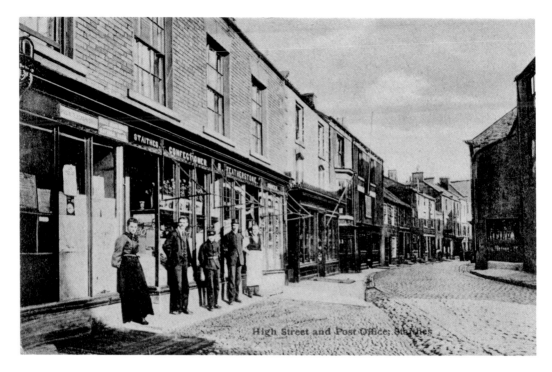

High Street and Post Office, Staithes

Staithes — the High Street

Down in the picturesque village of Staithes we see the old post office on the left, with two of the postmen posing with the staff of Featherstone's shop, which sold groceries and confectionery. The street area is entirely cobbled, and passing traffic clearly presents no problem for the residents, unlike the congestion that can occur today. An art gallery now lies on the left.

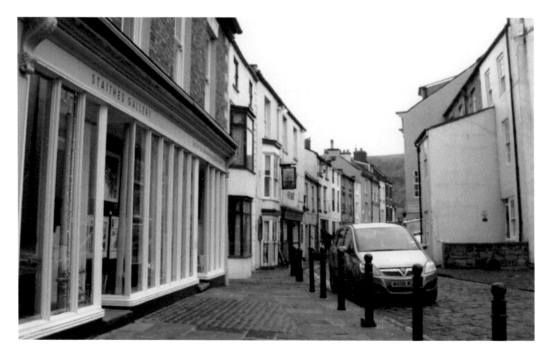

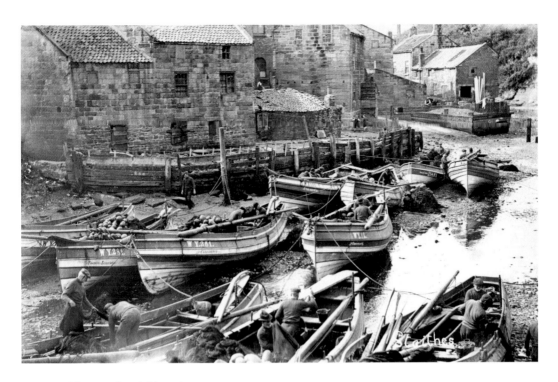

Staithes — the Fishing Fleet

A spectacular postcard of cobles drawn up the beck at Staithes, confirming what a busy fishing port the village was before the First World War. There are fishermen in each boat, preparing their gear for the task ahead. The photographer was Henry Charles Morley, who produced some amazing local postcards from his studio in the village. Very few people here now depend on fishing for their living.

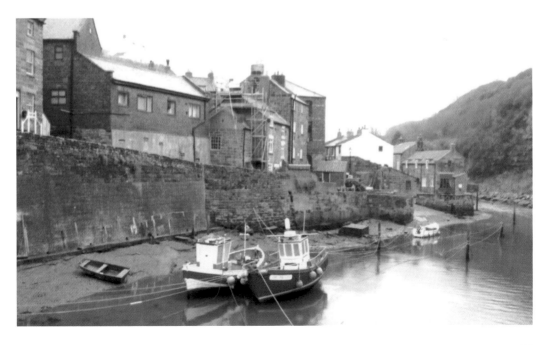

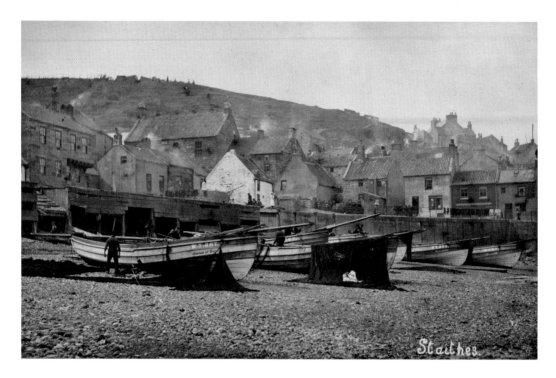

Staithes Harbour with Cobles

More fishing cobles drawn up the beach in the harbour at Staithes. The boats carry Whitby registration numbers, and include the *Anchor of Hope* and the *Friendship*. Many of the names had been passed down in families and were either sentimental or of a religious nature. The nets are drying in this Morley postcard. Cobles are in scarce supply at Staithes today.

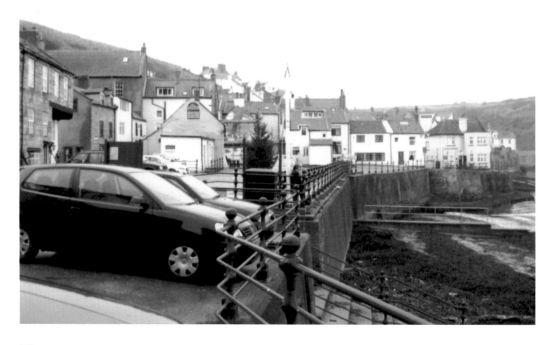

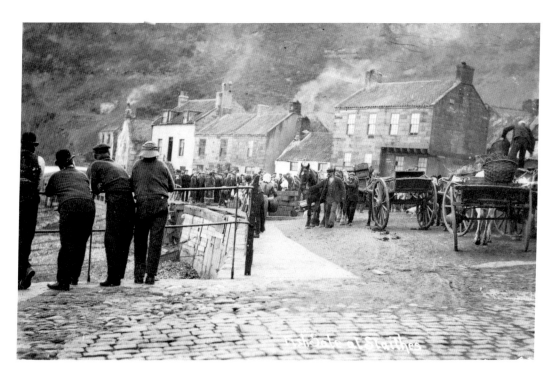

Staithes — the Fish Market

Fresh fish was landed each day in the small harbour of Staithes, and sold at the quayside to main dealers and travelling fish salesmen. It was certainly fresh! Here we see in this Morley view pony traps ready to take fish to the moorland villages. Staithes was as busy a fishing port as Whitby at this time. There is less atmosphere in the present day scene, but the lack of smoky chimneys is probably seen as an improvement.

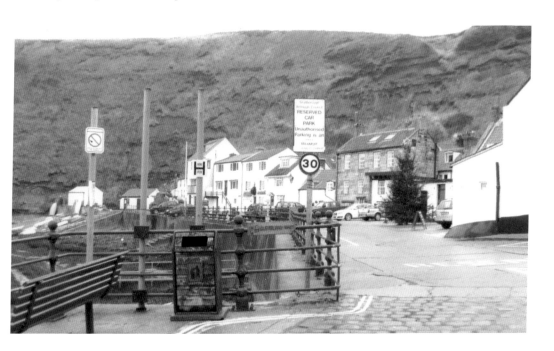

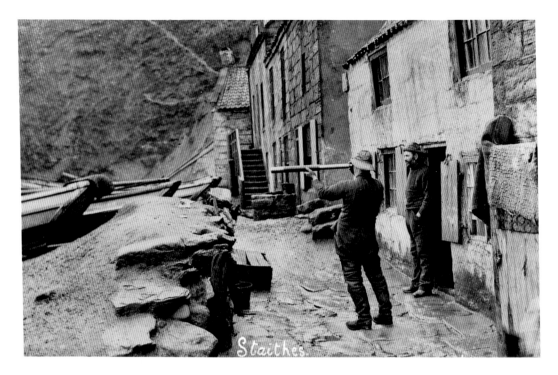

Staithes — the Fishermen

Another H. C. Morley postcard, somewhat posed but certainly not without interest. Two of the Staithes fishermen in their souwesters, dark blue 'ganseys' (jerseys) and sea boots look out to sea from the harbour side with the help of a telescope. Probably not part of their normal sea-going equipment, but it makes an impressive picture. The houses are still recognisable today.

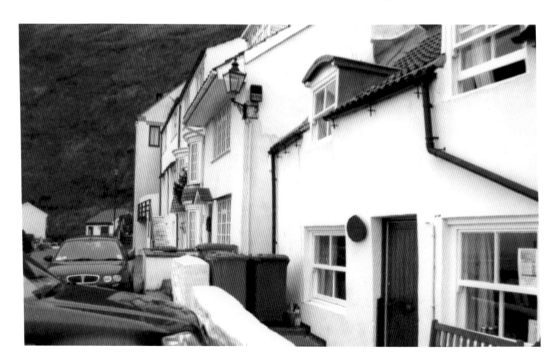

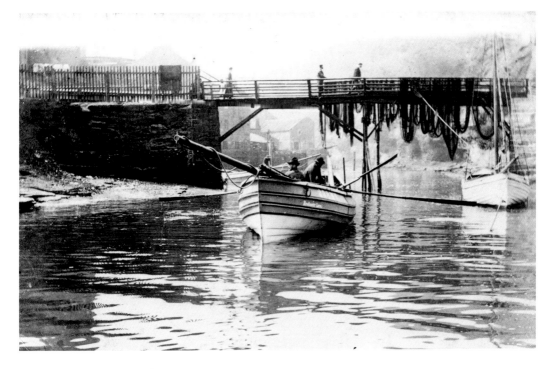

Staithes — the Beck

A tranquil postcard view of the Beck at high tide in Staithes, posted in May 1905. The coble is the *Brotherly Love*, registered in Whitby and appearing to be setting out on a fishing expedition. The drying nets on the old wooden footbridge between the Staithes and Cowbar communities add atmosphere to this Morley photograph. The footbridge has no doubt been replaced a number of times over the years. The cobles used oars and a sail to reach the fishing grounds.

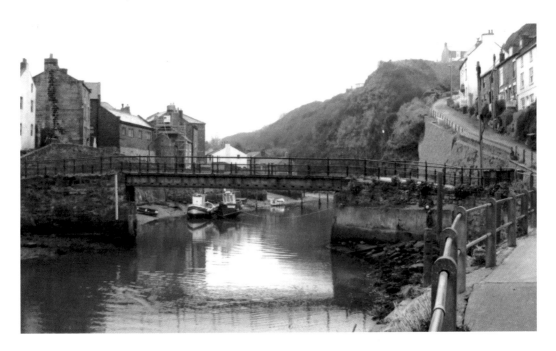

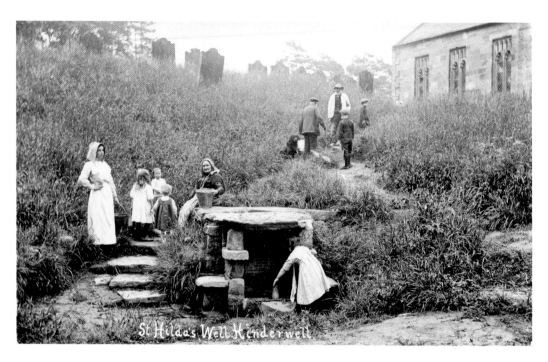

Hinderwell — St Hilda's Well

A beautiful period postcard by H. C. Morley of the churchyard at Hinderwell, the place name believed to have arisen from the St Hilda's Well, here illustrated. St Hilda was the first Abbess at Whitby Abbey, from AD 657 to AD 680. Carrying water from the local well was a requirement well known to our ancestors but nevertheless a hard, thankless task. Grass cutting was seen as a lesser priority! The well was renovated in 1912 by Hilda Palmer of Grinkle Park.

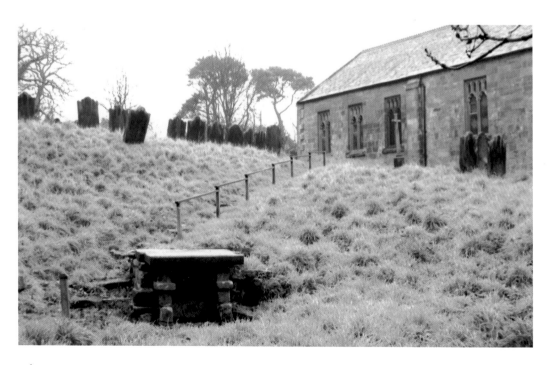

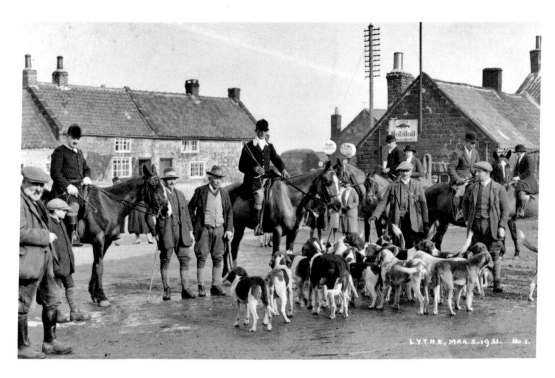

Lythe — the Hunt

A gathering of the Eskdale Hunt in the Square at Lythe in March 1931. The farmers all wear their traditional breeches, boots and gaiters. Hunting has more recently become a different activity, but remains very popular. Against the wall of the blacksmith's workshop can be seen pumps dispensing Pratt's petrol (later Esso) and an enamel Mobiloil advertising sign is prominent.

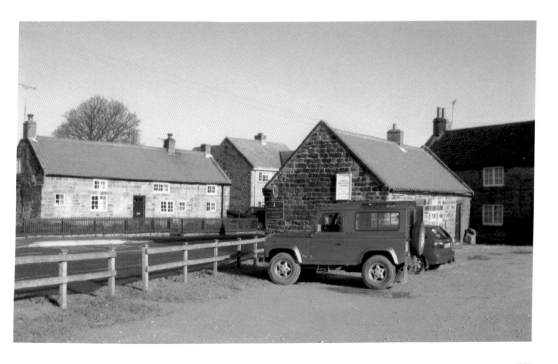

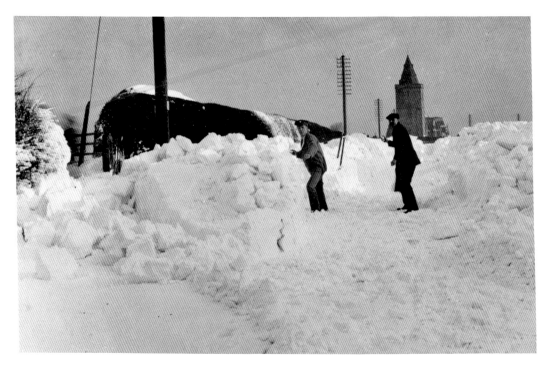

Lythe — a Winter Scene

Heavy snow in January 1918 completely blocked the main road between Lythe village and the parish church. The shovels seem quite inadequate for the task, and the workmen are aiming snowballs at the local photographer, Tom Watson. The church had been completely re-built shortly before the First World War, including a new design of a tower with an added spire, as illustrated here.

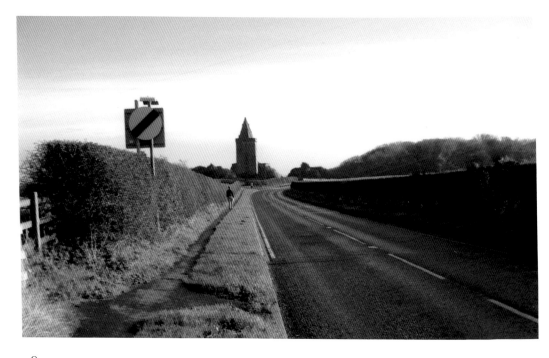

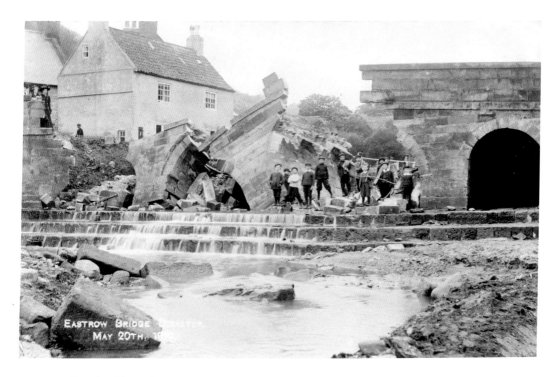

Sandsend Bridge Disaster

A severe local storm in the Lythe area in May 1910 led to a flash flood that carried massive tree debris down the river from Mulgrave Woods. The water power destroyed the familiar bridge at East Row in Sandsend, and this postcard view shows the local lads getting their moment of fame with the photographer. This is normally a safe play area for children at the edge of the beach, and an important route into Whitby from the moors.

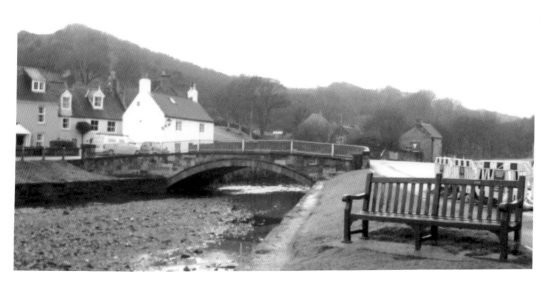

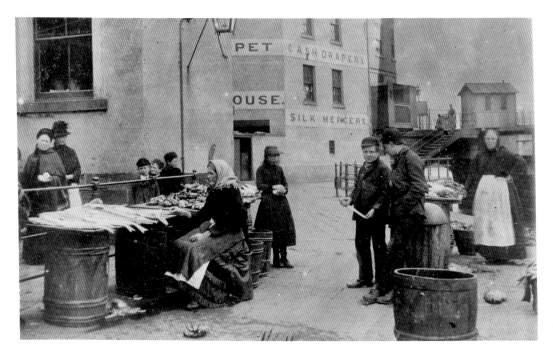

Whitby Fish Stall

The most important postcard photographer in Whitby before the First World War was John Thomas Ross, whose street studies of daily life and people are an important record of life a century ago. This early view of fish stalls near the old harbour bridge is a very collectable postcard. The nearby buildings were demolished as part of the 'Boots Corner' improvement some forty years ago. The premises of R. Grey and Company, 'Cash Drapers and Silk Mercers', can be seen in the background. Today's scene could not be more different.

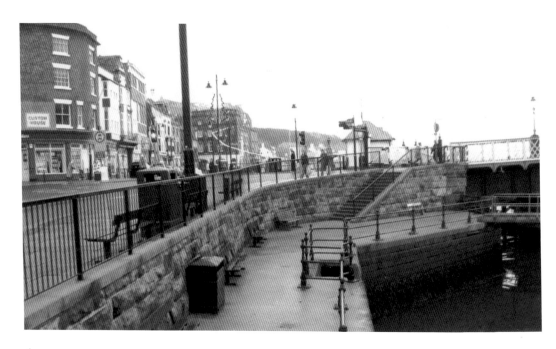

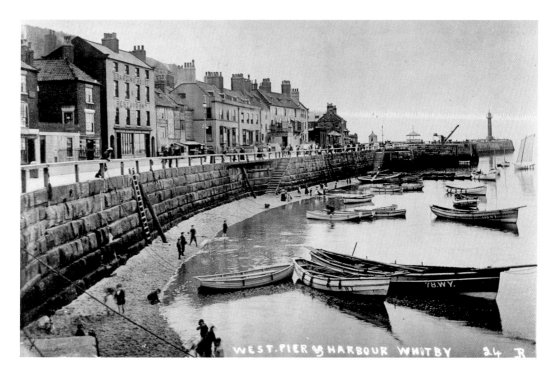

Whitby Quayside

Another early Ross postcard showing the quayside before all the wooden outward extensions into the harbour area were made to accommodate the busy fish trade. Without dredging, the harbour water level was shallower, and children can be seen on the sand at the water's edge. Modern buildings have now cluttered this lovely scene.

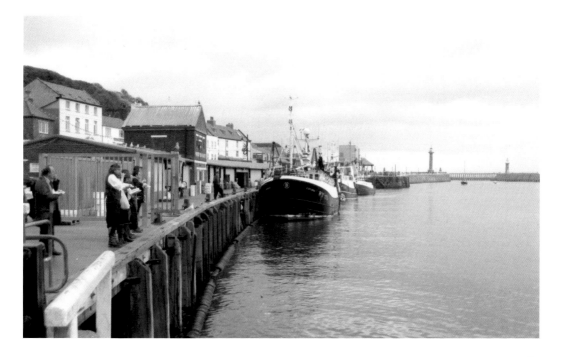

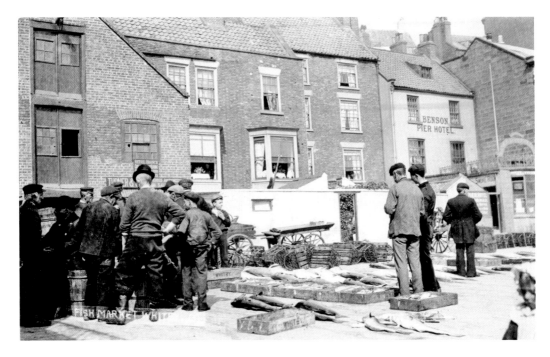

Whitby Fish Auction
A close-up of the outdoor fish market at Coffee House End, next to the Marine Hotel on the harbour side. Behind the men on the left can be seen the offices of the fish auctioneers, the family of Turner, who held that role for some generations. The Pier Hotel on the early view is still there, somewhat modified.

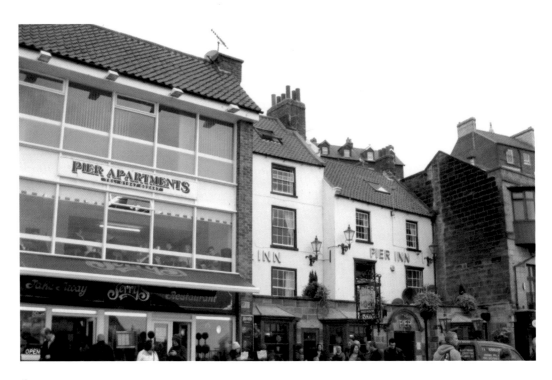

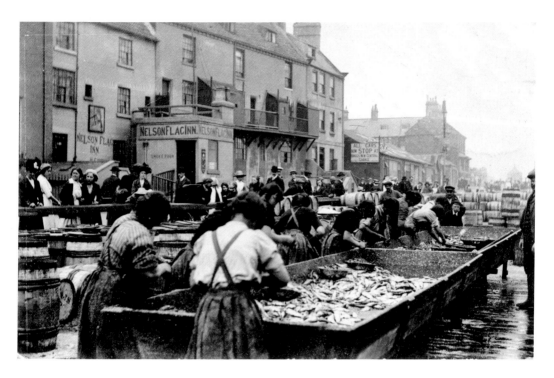

Whitby — the Herring Catch

Further along the quayside, and posted in 1913, the early view shows the Scottish girls who followed the Scottish fishing boats down the East Coast in July and August in search of the herring shoals. They are gutting the fresh herring before tightly packing them with salt into wooden barrels for transportation across Britain and even for export abroad. The Nelson Flag Inn licensee at this time was Henry Goodwill, but this street frontage has since undergone significant changes.

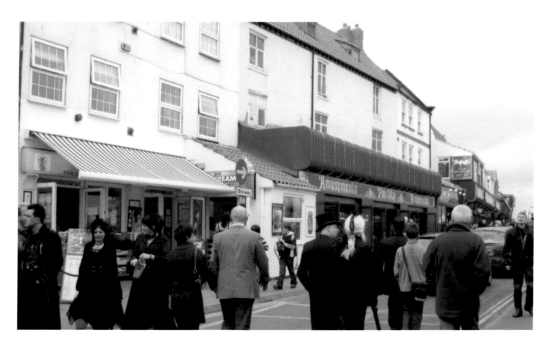

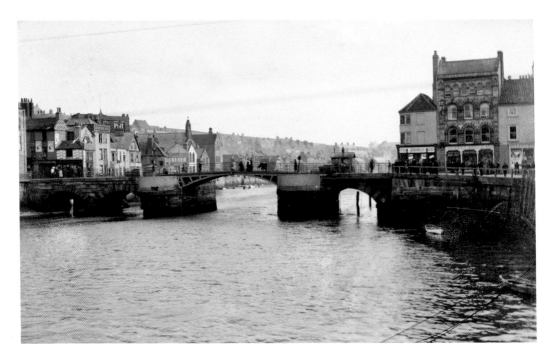

Whitby — the Old Bridge

Here is a clear view of the old Whitby Bridge, opened in 1835 and later replaced by the present swing bridge in 1909. It was an unpopular structure, having a navigable centre span of only 45 feet. This restricted the ship builders' designs in the upper harbour, and the bridge also suffered collision damage from those bigger ships which were just able to pass through the gap. Celebrations in August 2009 marked the centenary of today's familiar bridge.

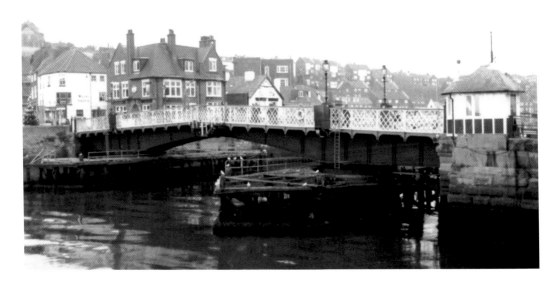

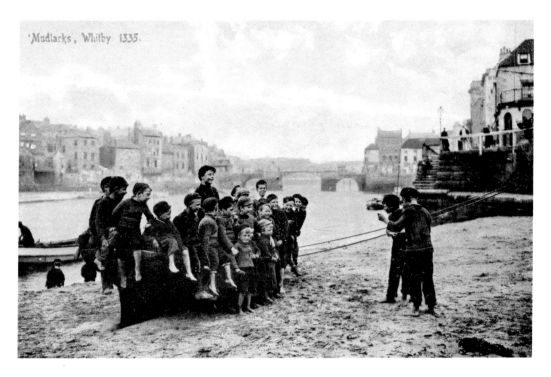

'Mudlarks, Whitby 1335.

Whitby Mudlarks

A charming view of children on the harbour sands in the days when the lack of dredging exposed large areas of the harbour bottom at low tide. Many of the boys are smiling — an unusual feature in early photographs. Taken about 1905, with the old bridge still in place. There must be grandchildren of these boys still living in Whitby. It is now impossible to stand in the same place!

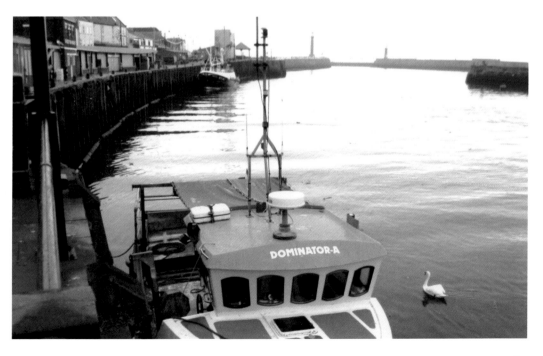

DOMINATOR-A

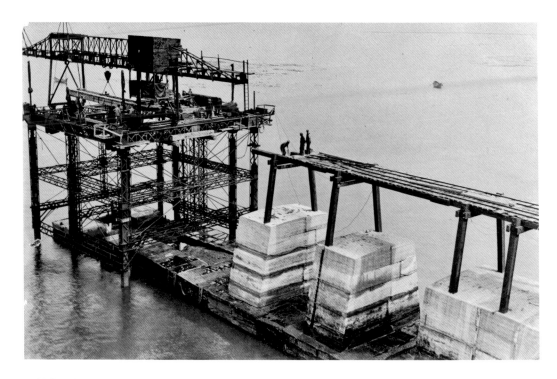

Whitby Pier Extensions

Another Ross postcard, of the building of the two pier extensions at Whitby harbour in 1913, which significantly improved the shelter offered to shipping. The special construction devices feature in a number of postcards of the time and were able to build the pier foundations under the sea. Known as the 'Iron Man' or 'Walking Man', they were occasionally capsized by heavy seas. Currently there is concern at the structural condition of the extensions after nearly a hundred years.

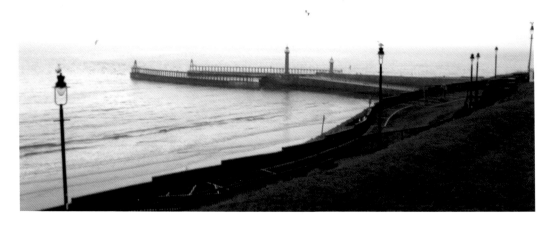

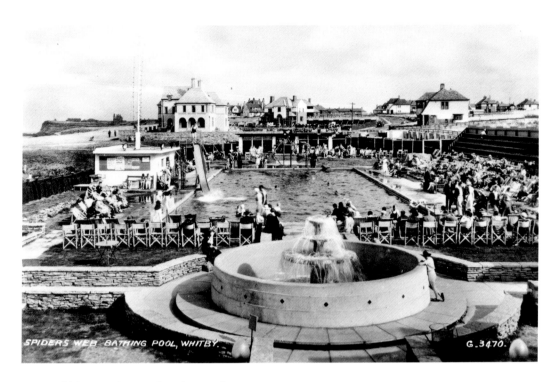

Whitby Outdoor Swimming Pool

On the cliff edge out towards Upgang, the Spider's Web outdoor swimming pool probably operated up to the 1950s and was — from personal experience — the coldest water ever known to man! Perhaps our climate was never really suited to such open-air pools. In its day, however, it was a very popular attraction for both visitors and local residents. Today, the only maintenance required for this area is some regular grass cutting.

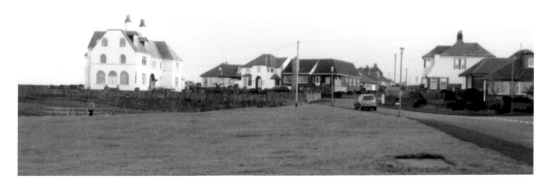

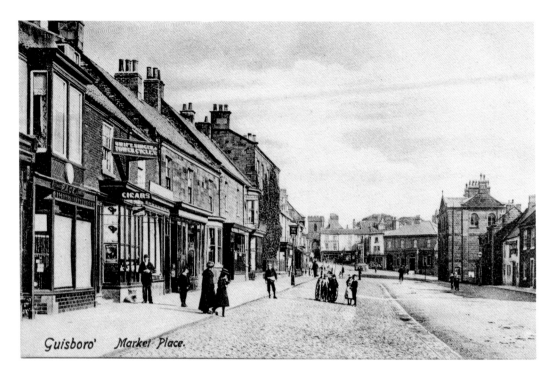

Guisborough Market Place

A view of the market place area in the High Street at Guisborough from February 1905. Not a car in sight — just a handcart on the cobbles in the centre. A bicycle shop on the left sells Swifts, Singer and Tower cycles. The parish church can just be seen in the distance. The town is much bigger now and a great deal busier! The tall building on the right is the town hall, dating from 1821.

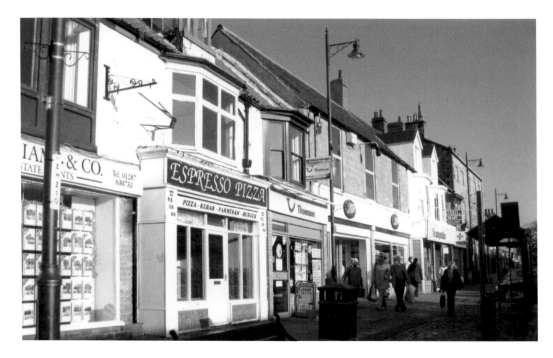

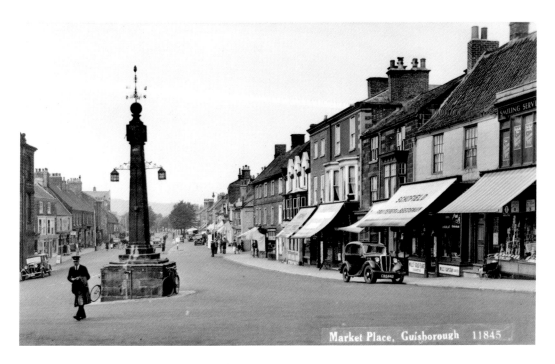

Market Place, Guisborough 11845

The Cross, Guisborough Market Place

The ancient cross is an imposing feature at the east end of the High Street. This postcard view from the 1930s looks along Westgate, in the Middlesbrough direction. Traffic is again scarce, with a bus in the distance and just a very few cars, the nearest being a Morris 8 parked on the right outside Schofields greengrocery shop ('Fruiterer and Seedsman'). As with many of our local market towns, the motor car has now become too prolific for comfort.

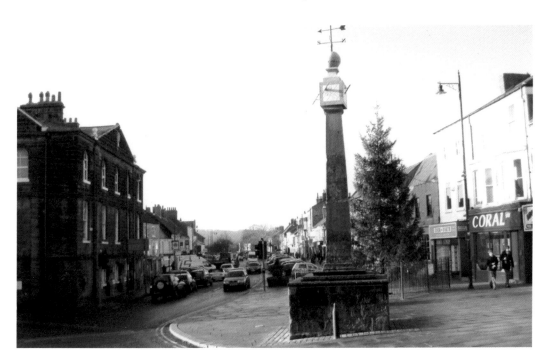

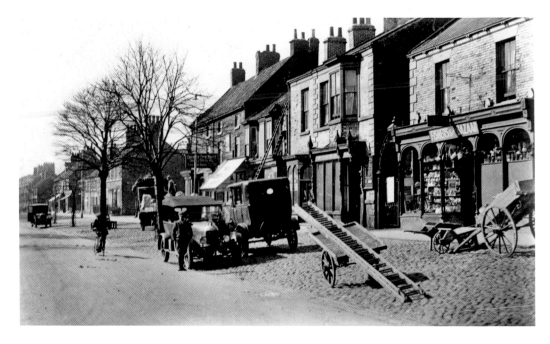

Guisborough — Fishers Bazaar

An interesting collection in Westgate, Guisborough. Outside Fishers Bazaar we find two wooden wheelbarrows, two handcarts and a substantial ladder — probably items for sale. Two interesting early motor cars are parked on the cobbles, and trees add variety to this street scene.

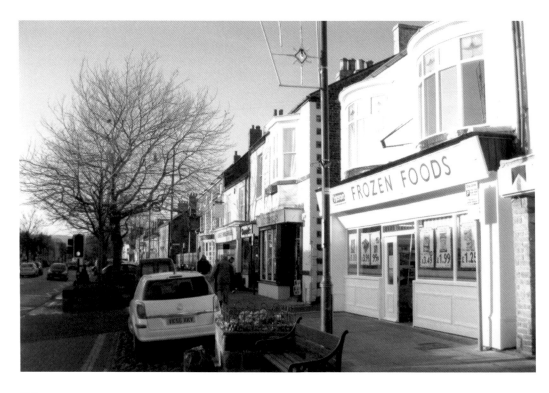

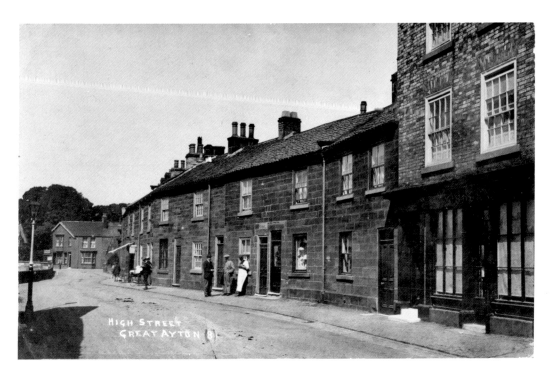

Great Ayton — High Street

A view at the West End of Great Ayton High Street in about 1905, with the traditional stone built terraced cottages in evidence. The River Leven is off to the left, and the bridge to Stokesley just out of sight at the far left. A shopkeeper in his white apron passes the time of day with some friends on the pavement. This is now a road with serious traffic congestion on occasions.

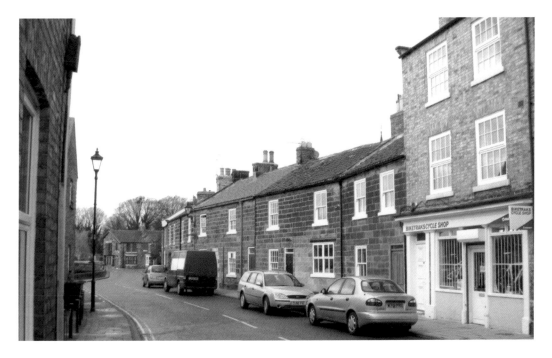

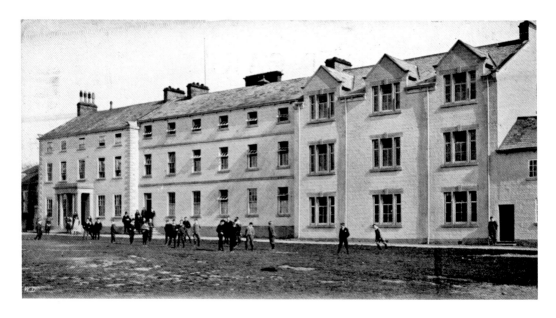

Great Ayton — The Friends' School

About 1910, the Friends' School at Great Ayton had a promotional series of postcards published, showing at least two-dozen different views of the school buildings and the teaching activities. This example shows some of the older boys relaxing on the High Green in front of the main school building. Sadly, like a number of fee-paying schools in modern times, the Friends' School closed through economic circumstances in 1997 and was subsequently converted into living apartments with executive homes also built in the grounds behind the main block.

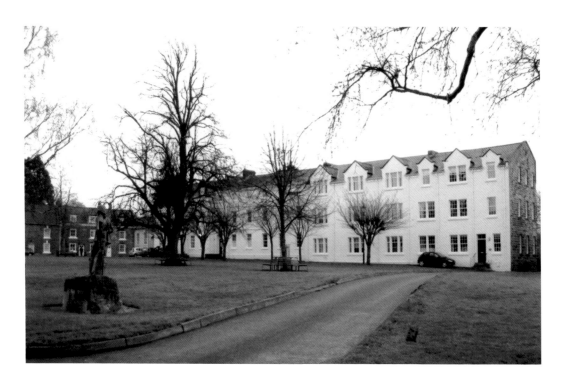

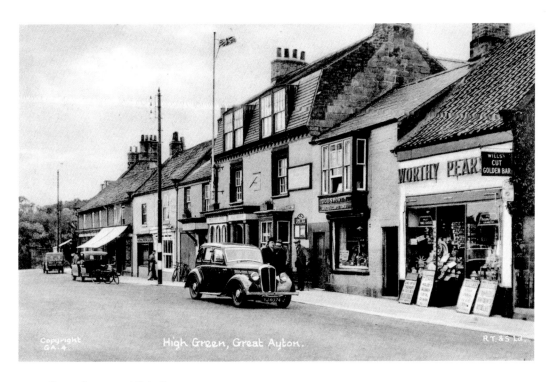

Great Ayton — High Green

The Royal Oak Hotel stands in the centre behind an elegant 1930's motor car, with other early vehicles parked by the distant shops. Worthy Pearson is still a shop name in the village. The hotel flies the Union flag, and across the road is the High Green, with the Friends' School beyond it.

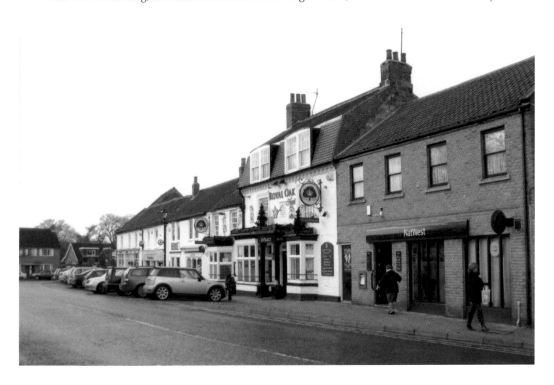

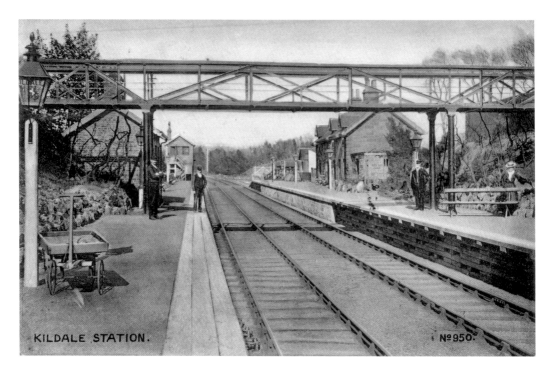

KILDALE STATION.   Nº950.

Kildale Station

A Brittain and Wright (of Stockton) postcard of the station at Kildale, at the head of the Esk Valley, in 1908. This was a well-kept and busy station on the Middlesbrough to Whitby line, employing several staff and serving a wide rural area. Like many of the smaller railway stations which have at least survived, it is today a shadow of its former self and a bit depressing.

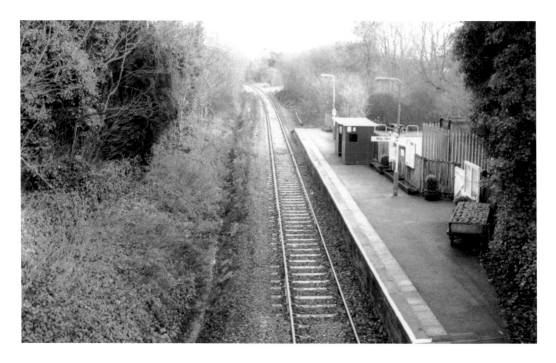

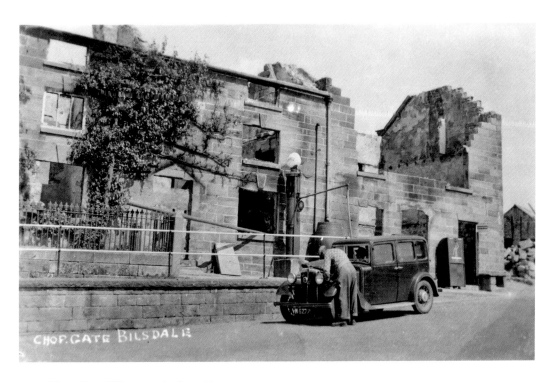

Chop Gate Village — Serious Fire

On 7 January 1938, a serious fire destroyed the shop and café at Chop Gate village, but miraculously spared the petrol store and the adjacent police house, and the chapel to the rear. Repairs to the car seen here evidently took precedence over the premises re-build! Comparing this picture with the next one, it is clear that larger windows were installed in the reconstruction.

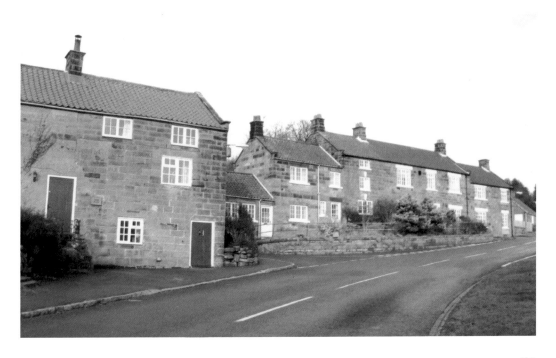

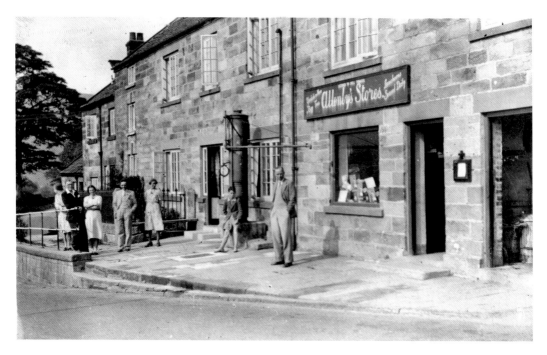

Chop Gate — Mrs Allenby's Stores

Mrs Allenby's shop at Chop Gate had one of the old swing-over petrol pumps to reach the passing cars, and also offered 'Yorkshire Ham and Egg Teas'. Situated at the entrance to the beautiful Bilsdale valley, it was a very popular watering place. The early picture here was probably taken in 1939, after the building was restored following the disastrous fire.

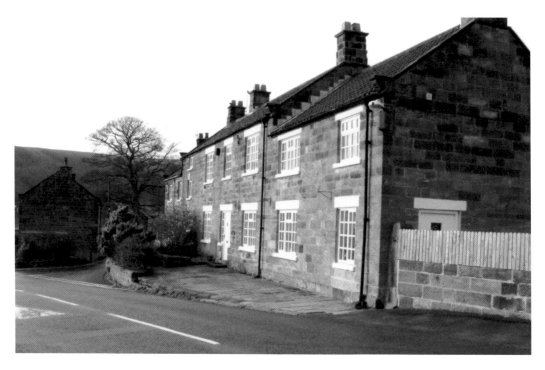

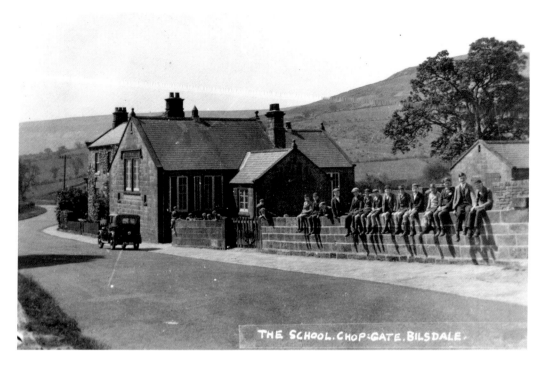

Chop Gate Village School, Bilsdale

Serving a very rural area of the North Yorkshire Moors, the present school at Chop Gate has played an important part in the local community since it was built in 1910. At one time there were up to seventy pupils attending — little more than twenty primary school age children today — and it would often close at busy farming times and in severe weather. The older boys pose on the wall for the view from the 1930s.

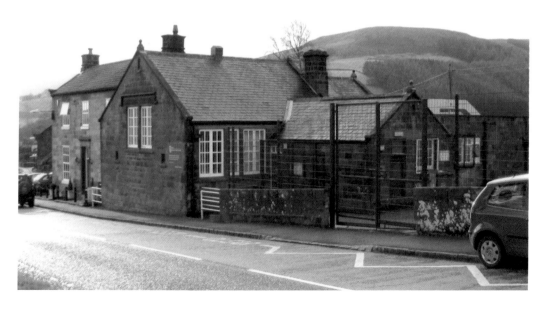

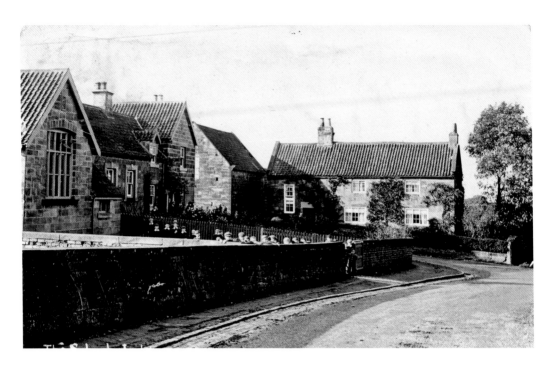

Ingleby Greenhow Village School

Posted in 1908, the young children of the village school in Ingleby Greenhow look over the playground wall at the photographer. Many of the boys wear the large Eton collars, which were very much of the period. This school was replaced elsewhere in the village by a modern building in 1972, and the original building converted into accommodation. In its own way the village is as remote as Chop Gate, and the school attendance would have been affected by the farming year and by severe weather.

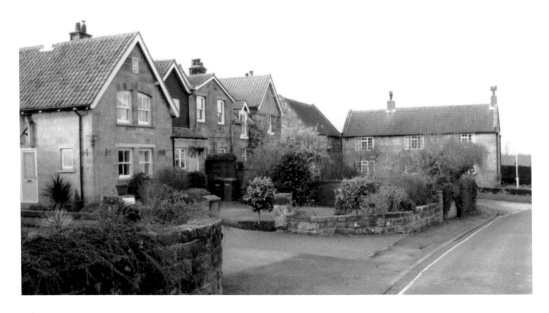

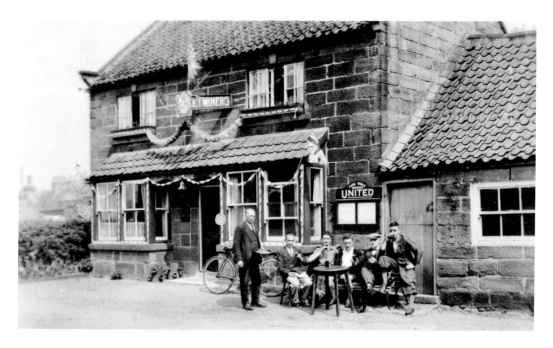

Great Broughton — the Jet Miners Inn

The caption on the early postcard has been accidentally reversed, but it reads 'Great Broughton Jubilee Celebrations', and a plaque attached to the Jet Miners Inn sign confirms it to be the 25th anniversary of the reign of George V in 1935. It remains a popular pub today. Many of the local bus services were then run by the United Automobile Company, and their bus timetable can be seen on the wall. The men are raising their glasses!

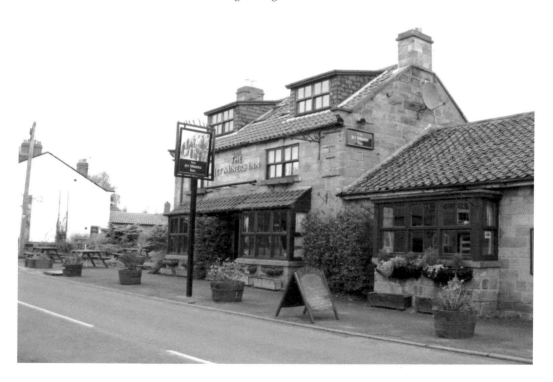

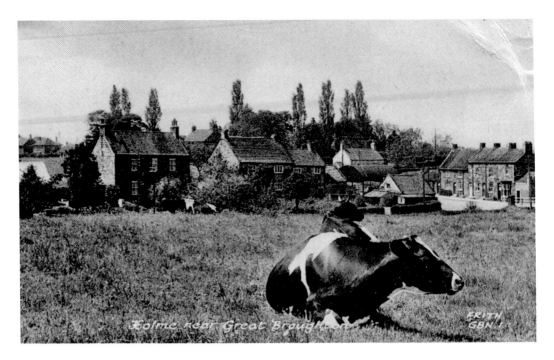

Great Broughton — the Village Green

The postcard was dated 1957, and shows the village green in Great Broughton, with cows in the foreground and the houses of The Holme in the background along the river. Very sadly, planning permission was inexplicably given for housing to be built on this valuable open space many years ago and the modern view shows the result. It was surely an appalling decision, but one not possible to reverse.

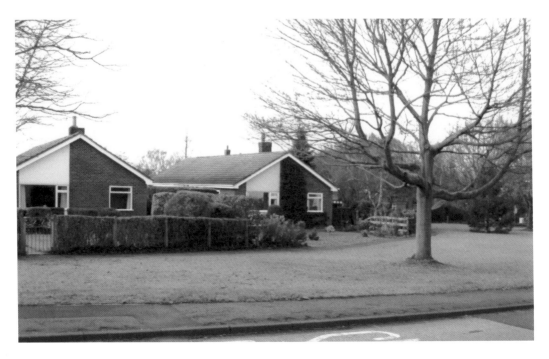

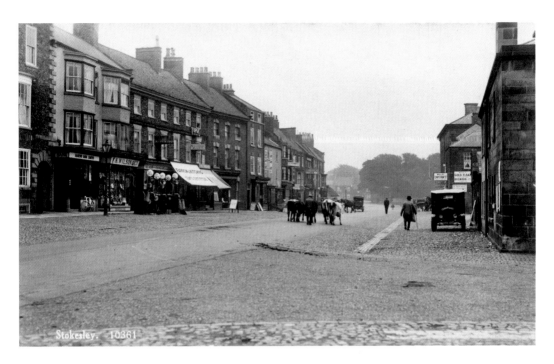

Stokesley — the High Street Looking East

A very quiet scene in Stokesley High Street, posted in 1930. Martins Bank on the left with the bay windows, next to F. K. Wilson & Co. where the five Pratts petrol pumps can be seen. Beyond that, the famous Gents Outfitters and department store of Farrow and Kitching. A man is driving his cows along the street, undisturbed by any passing traffic. Compare the bustle and congestion of life today!

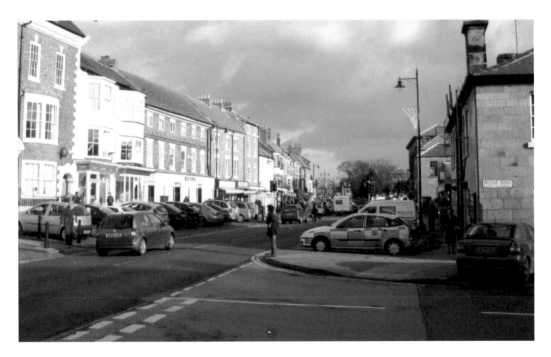

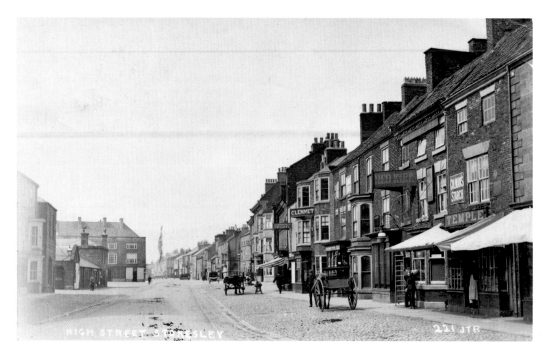

Stokesley — The High Street Looking West

Looking along the High Street in the opposite direction some twenty years earlier. Neither cars nor petrol pumps! The horse was still the essential element in public transport. We see the variety of three-storey period properties, which had developed along an unusually wide street over the previous 150 years. These broad, cobbled high streets are a unique feature of many historic North Yorkshire market towns. Again, it is impossible to get a car-free photograph today.

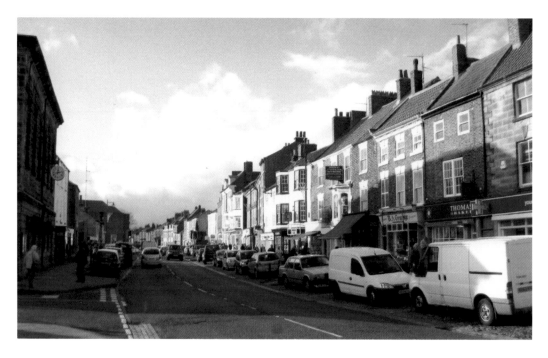

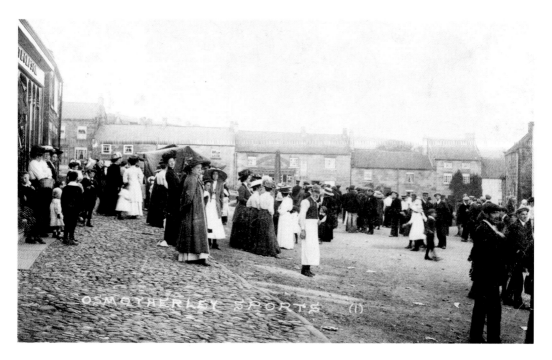

Osmotherley Village Sports

Always a very popular occasion, the origin of the Osmotherley Games goes back into the mists of history but they have always been eagerly anticipated in early July. The ladies always made a special effort to impress with their outfits. The historic and famous Thompson's shop lies on the extreme left (it is still there today, but now, sadly, closed) and Mr Thompson himself can be seen in his white apron in the centre of this postcard from about 1905.

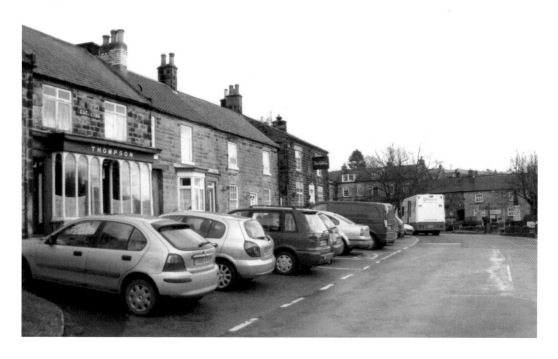

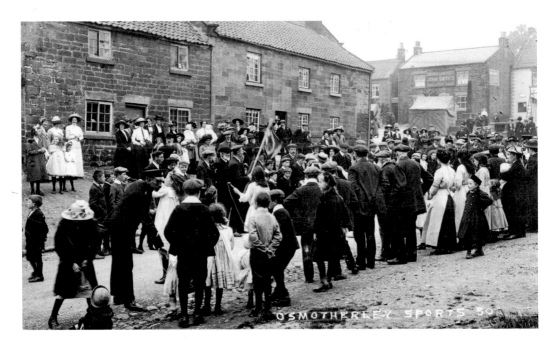

Osmotherley Village Sports

Another early view of the Osmotherley Sports, or Games, from the same period, looking up into the Village Square. The Market Cross can just be made out against the background of the Golden Lion Hotel. Young girls are skipping in the centre of the road — perhaps an endurance competition? Crowds still gather each year in the centre of the village for the Osmotherley Games, a testimony to their popularity.

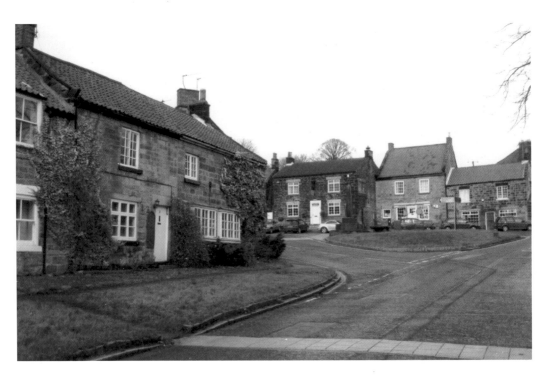